The Acceptable Sacrifice

The Excellency of a Broken Heart

by

John Bunyan

Fresh Bread

An imprint of

Destiny Image® Publishers, Inc.
P.O. Box 310
Shippensburg, PA 17257-0310

ISBN 0-7684-5004-7

For Worldwide Distribution
Printed in the U.S.A.

First Printing: 2001   Second Printing: 2001

This book and all other Destiny Image, Revival Press, MercyPlace, Fresh Bread, Destiny Image Fiction, and Treasure House books are available at Christian bookstores and distributors worldwide.

For a U.S. bookstore nearest you, call **1-800-722-6774**.
For more information on foreign distributors, call **717-532-3040**.
Or reach us on the Internet: **www.reapernet.com**

Endorsement

How has it come to pass, that in all times God's ministers have been made fearless as lions, and their brows have been firmer than brass; their hearts sterner than steel, and their words like the language of God? Why, it was simply for this reason; that it was not the man who pleaded, but it was God the Holy Ghost pleading through him. Have you never seen an earnest minister, with hands uplifted and eyes dropping tears, pleading with the sons of men? Have you never admired that portrait from the hand of old John Bunyan?—a grave person with eyes lifted up to heaven, the best of books in his hand, the law of truth written on his lips, the world behind his back, standing as if he pleaded with men, and a crown of gold hanging over his head. Who gave that minister so blessed a manner, and such goodly matter? Whence came his skill? Did he acquire it in the college? Did he learn it in the seminary? Ah, no. He learned it of the God of Jacob; he learned it of the Holy Ghost; for the Holy Ghost is the great counsellor who teaches us how to advocate his cause aright.

Rev. C.H. Spurgeon
From "The Comforter"
A Sermon (No.5) Delivered on Sabbath Evening, January 21, 1855,
at New Park Street Chapel, Southwark.

Contents

Preface

The Author of the ensuing Discourse (now with God, reaping the fruit of all his labour, diligence, and success in his Master's service) did experience in himself, through the grace of God, the nature, excellency, and comfort of a truly broken and contrite spirit: so that what is here written is but a transcript out of his own heart; for God, who had much work for him to do, was still hewing and hammering him by His Word, and sometimes also by more than ordinary temptations and desertions. The design, and also the issue thereof, through God's goodness, was the humbling and keeping of him low in his own eyes. The truth, as he acknowledged, is that he always needed the thorn in the flesh, and God, in mercy, sent it to him, lest, under his extraordinary circumstances, he should be exalted above measure, which, perhaps, was the evil that did more easily beset him than any other: but the Lord was pleased to overrule it to work for his good, and to keep him in that broken frame which is so acceptable unto Him, and concerning which it is said that He heals the broken in heart, and binds up their wounds, Ps. 147:3. It is a most necessary qualification, that should always be found in the disciples of Christ who are most eminent, and as stars of the first magnitude in the firmament of the church. Disciples in the highest form of profession need to be thus qualified in the exercise of every grace, and the performance of every duty. It is that which God does principally and more especially look after in all our approaches and accesses to Him. God will look to him, and dwell with him who is poor and of a contrite spirit, Isa. 57:15, and 66:2. And the reason why God will manifest so much respect to one so qualified, is, because he carries it so becomingly towards Him: he comes and lies at His feet, and discovers a quickness of sense, and apprehensiveness of whatever may be dishonourable and distasteful to God, Ps. 38:4. And if the Lord does at any time but shake His rod over him, he comes trembling, and kisses the rod, and says, "It is the Lord, let Him do what seemeth Him good," 1 Sam. 3:18. He is aware that he has sinned and gone astray like a lost sheep, and therefore will justify God in His severest proceedings against him.

This broken heart is also a pliable and flexible heart, and prepared to receive whatever impressions God shall make upon it, and is ready to be moulded into any frame that should best please the Lord. He says, with Samuel, "Speak, for thy servant heareth," 1 Sam. 3:10; and with David, "When Thou saidst, Seek ye My face; my heart said unto Thee, Thy face, Lord, will I seek," Ps. 27:8. And so with Paul, who tremblingly said, "Lord, what wilt Thou have me to do?" Acts 9:6.

Now, therefore, surely such a heart as this is very delightful to God. He says to us, "My son, give Me thine heart," Prov. 23:26; but, doubtless, He means there a broken heart. An unbroken heart we may keep to ourselves: it is the broken heart which God will have us to give to Him; for, indeed, it is all the amends that the best of us are capable of making for all the injury we have done to God in sinning against Him. We are not able to give better satisfaction for breaking God's laws than by breaking our own hearts: this is all we can do of that kind, for the blood of Christ only must give the due and full satisfaction to the justice of God for what provocations we are at any time guilty of; but all that we can do is to accompany the acknowledgments we make of miscarriages with a broken and contrite spirit. Therefore, we find that when David had committed those two foul sins of adultery and murder against God, he saw that all his sacrifices signified nothing to the expiating of his guilt; therefore he brings to God a broken heart, which carried in it the best expressions of indignation against himself, as of the highest respect he could show to God, 2 Cor. 7:11.

The day in which we live, and the present circumstances which the people of God and these nations are under, do loudly proclaim a very great necessity of being in this broken and tender frame; for who can foresee what will be the issue of this violent unrest that is among us? Who knows what will become of the ark of God? Therefore it is a seasonable duty, with old Eli, to sit trembling for it. Do we not also hear the sound of the trumpet, the alarm of wars, and ought we not, with the prophet, to cry out, "My bowels, my bowels! I am pained at my very heart; my heart maketh a noise in me; I cannot hold my peace," etc. Jer 4:19. That holy man was affected with the consideration of what might befall Jerusalem, the temple and ordinances of God, etc., as the consequence of the present dark dispensations they were under. Will not a humble posture better become us when we have God's humbling activity before us? Mercy and judgment seem to be struggling in the same womb of Providence, and which will come first out we know not; but neither of them can we comfortably meet but with a broken and contrite spirit. If judgment comes, Josiah's posture of tenderness will be the best we can be found in; and also to say with David, "My flesh trembleth for fear of thee; and I am afraid of thy judgments," Ps. 119:120. It is very sad when God smites and we are not grieved, which the prophet complains of: "Thou hast stricken them, but they have not grieved," etc. "They have made their faces harder than a rock; they have refused to return," Jer. 5:3.

But those that know the power of His anger, will have a deep awe of God upon their hearts, and, observing Him in all His motions, will have the greatest apprehensions of His displeasure; so that when He is coming forth in any terrible dispensation, they will, according to their duty, prepare to meet Him with a humbled and broken heart: but if He should appear to us in His goodness, and further lengthen out the day of our peace and liberty, yet still the contrite frame will be most seasonable; then will be a proper time, with Job, to abhor ourselves in dust and ashes, Job 42:6, and to say with David, Who are we, that Thou hast brought us hitherto? 2 Sam. 7:18.

The Acceptable Sacrifice

But we must still know that this broken tender heart is not a plant that grows in our own soil, but is the peculiar gift of God himself. He that made the heart must break the heart: we may be under heart-breaking divine activity, and yet the heart remain altogether unbroken, as it was with Pharaoh, whose heart, though it was under the hammers of ten terrible judgments immediately succeeding one another, yet continued hardened against God. The heart of man is harder than hardness itself, till God softens and breaks it: because men move not, they relent not, therefore God must thunder ever so terribly; let God in the greatest earnest cast abroad His firebrands, arrows, and death, in the most dreadful representations of wrath and judgment, yet still man trembles not, nor is any more astonished than if, in all this, God were but in jest, till He comes and falls to work with him, and forces him to cry out, What have I done? what shall I do?

Therefore let us have recourse to Him, who, as he gives the new heart, so also therewith the broken heart. And let men's hearts be never so hard, if God comes once to deal effectually with them, they shall become mollified and tender, as it was with those hardened Jews who, by wicked and cruel hands, murdered the Lord of life: though they insulted Him a great while, yet how suddenly, when God brought them under the hammer of His Word and Spirit, in Peter's powerful ministry, were they broken, and, being pricked in their hearts, cried out, "Men and brethren, what shall we do?" Acts 2:37.

And in the same way we have in the jailor, who was a most barbarous, hard-hearted wretch; yet, when God came to deal with him, he was soon tamed, and his heart because exceeding soft and tender, Acts 16:29,30.

Men may speak long enough, and the heart not at all be moved; but, the voice of the Lord is powerful; the voice of the Lord is full of majesty, and breaks the rocks and cedars: He turns the rock into a standing water, the flint into a fountain of waters, Ps. 29:4-5; Ps. 114:8. And this is a glorious work indeed, that hearts of stone should be dissolved and melted into waters of godly sorrow, working repentance not to be repented of, 2 Cor. 7:10.

Preface

When God speaks with great effect, the stoutest heart must melt and yield. Wait upon God, then, for the softening of thy heart, and avoid whatsoever may be a means of hardening it; as the apostle cautions the Hebrews. "Take heed, lest any of you be hardened through the deceitfulness of sin," Heb. 3:13.

Sin is deceitful, and will harden all those that indulge it. The more a man is drawn to his lust, the more he will be hardened by it. There is a natural hardness in every man's heart; and though it may be softened by the gospel, yet, if that softening be neglected, the heart will fall to its native hardness again, as it is with the wax and the clay.

Therefore, how much does it behoove us to keep close to God in the use of all the gospel power, whereby our hearts, being once softened, may be always kept so; which is best done by repeating the use of those means which at first blessed us by softening our hearts.

The following treatise may be of great use to the people of God, with His blessing accompanying it, to keep their hearts tender and broken, when so many, after their hardness and impenitent heart, are treasuring up wrath against the day of wrath, Rom. 2:5.

Oh, let none who peruse this book herd with that generation of hardened ones, but be a companion of all those that mourn in Zion, and whose hearts are broken for their own, the church's, and the nation's sins; who, indeed, are the only likely ones that will stand in the gap to divert judgments. When Shishak, king of Egypt, with a great host, came up against Judah, having taken their frontier fenced cities, they sat down before Jerusalem, which put them all under a great consternation; the king and princes, upon this, humbled themselves: the Lord sends a gracious message to them by Shemaiah the prophet, the import whereof was, that because they humbled themselves, the Lord would not destroy them, nor pour out His wrath upon them by the hand of Shishak, 2 Chron. 12:5-7.

The greater the party of mourning Christians, the more hope we have that the storm impending may be blown over, and the blessings enjoyed may yet continue. As long as there is a grieving party, we may hope to be yet preserved; at least such will have the mark set upon themselves which shall distinguish them from those whom the slaughtermen shall receive commission to destroy, Ezek. 9:4.

But I shall no more enlarge the porch, as designing a way for the reader's entrance into the house, where, for sure, he will be pleased with the furniture and provision he finds in it. I shall only further assure him, that this whole book was not only prepared for, but also put unto the press by the author himself, whom the Lord was pleased to remove, to the great loss and inexpressible grief of many precious souls, before the sheets could be all removed from the press.

And now, as I hinted in the beginning, that what was transcribed out of the author's heart into the book, may be transcribed out of the book into the hearts of all who shall peruse it, is the desire and prayer of a lover and honourer of all saints, as such,

George Cokayn
September 21, 1688

Foreword

The Acceptable Sacrifice was printed four years after the death of John Bunyan. He considered it to be the culmination and the most important of all of his previous works. This book has had a dramatic impact on my own personal life and understanding of the Christian's pursuit of God. In my book, *The God Chasers*, I wrote, "When His presence becomes so strong that you are oblivious to everyone and everything else around you, then healing can come in an encounter with God from which you will never recover. Your heart will be as permanently *disabled* with love as Jacob's leg was left with a limp!" I borrowed that word 'disabled' directly from this writing of John Bunyan. He describes a broken heart as one that is disabled so that it no longer runs after the former things.

Bunyan persuasively proves the magnificence of a broken heart. With spiritual sensitivity and in a meticulous manner he carefully unveils the splendor and attraction of a heart that has been broken by the Lord. Bunyan calls the broken in heart God's beloved, His jewels.

This book is not for the spiritually faint at heart. It will leave you squirming as the intensity of its convincing words and compelling language beats constantly upon the shores of your soul. You will be tempted to throw the book down but if you are careful to listen, a deep cry within you will whisper faintly, "I must wound you before I can heal you."

In *The God Chasers* I wrote concerning Moses, "He longed for more than *visitation*; his soul longed for *habitation*." Bunyan makes it so dramatically obvious that the broken heart is to become a habitation for the Spirit of God.

A broken heart fits with the heart of God. God covets to dwell with the broken in heart and the broken in heart desires His communion.

"Wherefore, here is the point, come broken, come contrite, come aware of and sorry for your sins, or your coming will be counted as no coming to God at all." Only the broken hearted can chase after God. It is the limp of the broken that qualifies one to enter the race. This book is a training manual for those who would chase after God.

Tommy Tenney
Author, GodChaser

Chapter 1

The Excellency of a Broken Heart

The sacrifices of God are a broken spirit: a broken and a contrite heart, O God, Thou wilt not despise. (Psalms 51:17)

THIS Psalm is David's penitential Psalm. It may be fitly so called, because it is a Psalm by which is manifest the unfeigned sorrow which he had for his horrible sin, in defiling of Bathsheba, and slaying Uriah her husband; a relation at large of which you have in the 11th and 12th of the second of Samuel.

This Psalm reveals that this poor man had mercy dealing in his heart, as soon as conviction fell upon his spirit. While he cries for mercy, then he confesses his heinous offenses, then he bewails the depravity of his nature; sometimes he cries out to be washed and sanctified, and then again he is afraid that God will cast him away from His presence, and take His Holy Spirit utterly from him: and thus he goes on till he comes to the text, and there he fixes his mind, finding in himself that heart and spirit which God did not dislike: "The sacrifices of God," says he, "are a broken spirit"; as if he should say, I thank God I have that. "A broken and a contrite heart," says he, "O God, Thou wilt not despise"; as if he should say, I thank God I have that.

1

The Acceptable Sacrifice

The words consist of two parts:

1.   An Assertion.

2.   A Demonstration of that Assertion.

The Assertion is this, "The sacrifices of God are a broken spirit."

The Demonstration is this, "Because a broken and a contrite heart God will not despise."

In the Assertion, we have two things that present themselves to our consideration: 1. That a broken spirit is to God a sacrifice. 2. That it is to God as that which answers to or goes beyond all sacrifices: "The sacrifices of God are a broken spirit." The demonstration of this is plain, for *that* heart God will not despise; "a broken and a contrite heart, O God, Thou wilt not despise."

From which I draw this conclusion, That a spirit rightly broken, a heart truly contrite, is to God an excellent thing; that is, a thing that goes beyond all external duties whatever; for that is intended by this saying, "The sacrifices," because it answereth to all sacrifices which we can offer to God: yes, it serves in the room of all: all our sacrifices without this are nothing; this alone is all.

There are four things that are very acceptable to God.

First is, The sacrifice of the body of Christ for our sins; of this you read, Heb. 10; for there you have it preferred to all burnt offerings and sacrifices; it is this that pleases God; it is this that sanctifies and so sets the people acceptable in the sight of God.

Secondly, genuine love to God is counted better than all sacrifices, or external parts of worship; "And to love [the Lord thy God] with all the heart, and with all the understanding, and with all the soul, and with all the strength, and to love his neighbour as himself, is more than all whole burnt offerings and sacrifices," Mark 12:33.

Thirdly, To walk holy and humbly and obediently towards and before God, is another: Mic. 6:6-8. "Hath the Lord as great delight in burnt offerings and sacrifices, as in obeying the voice of the Lord? Behold, to obey is better than sacrifice, and to hearken than the fat of rams," 1 Sam. 15:22.

Fourthly, And this in our text is the fourth, "The sacrifices of God are a broken spirit: a broken and a contrite heart, O God, thou wilt not despise."

But note by the way, that this broken, this broken and contrite heart, is thus excellent only to God: "O God," says he, "Thou wilt not despise it": by which is implied, the world does not have this esteem or respect for such a heart, or for one that is of a broken and a contrite spirit: no, no: a man, a woman, that is blessed with a broken heart is so far off from getting by that esteem with the world, that they are but burdens, and trouble houses wherever they are or go; such people carry with them torment and anxiety; they are in carnal families, as David was to the King of Gath, "troublers of the house," 1 Sam. 21.

Their sighs, their tears, their day and night groans, their cries and prayers and solitary carriages put all the carnal family out of order; hence you have them brow-beaten by some, condemned by others, yes, and their company fled from and deserted by others. But mark the text, "A broken and a contrite heart, O God, Thou wilt not despise," but rather accept; for not to despise is, with God, to esteem and set a high price upon.

But we will demonstrate by several particulars, that a broken spirit, a spirit rightly broken, a heart truly contrite, is to God an excellent thing.

The Broken Heart Is Better Than Sacrifices

First, This is evident from the comparison, "Thou desirest not sacrifice, else would I give it; Thou delightest not in burnt-offerings: the sacrifices of God are a broken spirit," etc., Isa. 51:16-17. Mark, He rejects sacrifices, offerings and sacrifices; that is, all Levitical ceremonies under the law, and all external performances under the gospel; but accepts a broken heart. It is therefore manifest by this, were there nothing else to be said, that proves, that a heart truly broken, truly contrite, is to God an excellent thing; for, as you see, such a heart is set before all sacrifice, and

3

yet they were the ordinances of God, and things that He commanded. But, lo! a broken spirit is above them all, a contrite heart goes beyond them, yea beyond them, when put all together. Thou wilt not have the one, Thou wilt not despise the other. O brethren! a broken and contrite heart is an excellent thing. Have I said, a broken heart, a broken and a contrite heart is esteemed above all sacrifice? I will add,

The Broken Heart Is Honored by God

Secondly, It is of greater esteem with God, than is either heaven or earth, and that is more than to be set before external duties. "Thus saith the Lord, The Heaven is My throne, and the earth is My footstool: where is the house that ye build unto Me? and where is the place of My rest? For all those things hath Mine hand made, and all those things have been, saith the Lord: but to this man will I look, even to him that is poor and of a contrite spirit, and trembleth at My word," Isa. 66:1,2. Note that God says He has made all these things; but He doth not say that He will look to them, that is, take complacency and delight in them; no, there is that wanting in all that He has made, and should take up and delight His heart: but now, let a broken-hearted sinner come before Him, yes, He searches the world to find such an one, and having found him, "To this man," says He, "will I look." I say again, that such a man, to Him, is of more value than is either heaven or earth: "They," says He, "wax old," they shall perish and vanish away; but this man, He continues, he (as is presented to us in another place under another character) "he shall abide for ever," Heb. 1:10-12; 1 John 2:17.

"To this man will I look," with this man will I be delighted; for so to look doth sometimes signify. "Thou hast ravished My heart, My sister, My spouse," saith Christ to his humble-hearted: "thou hast ravished My heart with one of thine eyes" (while it is as a conduit to let the rivers out of thy broken heart), I am taken, saith He, "with one chain of thy neck," Song 4:9. Here, you see, He looks and is ravished, He looks and is taken; as it saith in another place, "The king is held in the galleries," Song 7:5. That is, is taken with His beloved, "with the doves' eyes" of His beloved (1:15), with the contrite spirit of His people.

4

But it is not reported of Him with respect to heaven or earth; them He sets more lightly by; them He reserves unto fire against the day of judgment, and perdition of ungodly men, 2 Pet. 3:7. But the broken in heart are His beloved, His jewels.

Again what I have said as to this, must go for the truth of God, that a broken-hearted sinner, a sinner with a contrite spirit, is of more esteem with God than is either heaven or earth. He says, He has made them; but He does not say, He will look to them: He says, they are His throne and footstool; but He does not say, they have taken or ravished His heart; no, it is those that are of a contrite spirit that do this.

But the broken in heart are His beloved, His jewels.

But there is yet more in the words, "To this man will I look"; that is, For this man will I care; about this man will I camp; I will put this man under My protection; for so to look to one, does sometimes signify; and I take the meaning in this place to be such, Prov. 27:23; Jer. 39:12; 40:4.

"The Lord upholdeth all that fall, and raiseth up all those that be bowed down," Ps. 145:14. And the broken-hearted are of this number; wherefore He cares for, camps about, and has set His eyes upon such an one for good. This therefore is a second demonstration to prove that the man that has his spirit rightly broken, his heart truly contrite, is of great esteem with God.

God Dwells With the Broken Heart

Thirdly, yet further, God does not only prefer such an one, as has been said, before heaven and earth, but He loves, He desires to have that man for an intimate, for a companion: He must dwell, He must cohabit with him that is of a broken heart, with such as are of a contrite spirit. "For thus saith the high and lofty One that inhabiteth eternity, whose name is Holy, I dwell in the high and holy place, with him also that is of a contrite and humble spirit," Isa. 57:15.

Behold here both the majesty and condescension of the high and lofty One; His majesty, in that He is high, and the inhabiter of eternity.

5

"I am the high and lofty One," says He; "I inhabit eternity." This consideration is enough to make the broken-hearted man creep into a mousehole to hide himself from such a majesty. But behold His heart, His condescending mind: I am for dwelling also "with him that hath a broken heart, with him that is of a contrite spirit": that is the man that I would converse with, that is the man with whom I will cohabit, that is he, says God, I will choose for My companion. For to desire to dwell with one, supposes all these things; and truly, of all the men in the world, none have acquaintance with God, none understand what communion with Him, and what His teachings mean, but such as are of a broken and contrite heart: "The Lord is nigh unto them that are of a broken heart," Ps. 34:18. These are intended in the 14th Psalm, where it is said, "The Lord looked down from heaven...to see if there were any that did understand, and seek God" (14:2), that He might find somebody in the world with whom He might converse; for indeed there is none else that either understands, or that can attend to listen to Him. God is forced to break men's hearts, before He can make them willing to cry to Him, or be willing that He should have any concerns with them; the rest shut their eyes, stop their ears, withdraw their hearts, or say unto God, "Begone," Job 21. But now the broken heart can attend it, he has leisure, yes, leisure and will, and understanding and all; and therefore he is a fit man to have to do with God.

There is also room in this man's house, in this man's heart, in this man's spirit, for God to dwell, for God to walk, for God to set up a kingdom.

There is room in the house of the broken man for God to set up a Kingdom.

Here therefore is suitableness. "Can two walk together," saith God, "except they be agreed?" Amos 3:3. The broken-hearted desires God's company: "When wilt thou come unto me?" says he. The broken-hearted loveth to hear God speak and talk to him. Here is a suitableness: "Make me," says he, "to hear joy and gladness; that the bones which thou hast broken may rejoice," Ps. 51:8.

But here lies the glory, in that the high and lofty One, the God that inhabits eternity, and that has a high and holy place for His habitation,

6

should choose to dwell with, and to be a companion of the broken in heart, and of them that are of a contrite spirit: yea, and here is also great comfort for such.

God Reserves His Comfort and Compassion for the Broken Heart

Fourthly, God does not only prefer such a heart before all sacrifices, nor esteem such a man above heaven and earth, nor yet only desire to be of his acquaintance, but He reserves for him His chief comforts, His heart-reviving and soul-cherishing relief. I dwell, saith He, with such to revive them, and to support and comfort them, "to revive the spirit of the humble, and to revive the heart of the contrite ones," Isa. 57:15. The broken-hearted man is a fainting man; he has his qualms, his sinking fits; he often dies away with pain and fear; he must be stayed with flagons and comforted with apples, or else he cannot tell what to do. He pines, he pines away in his iniquity; nor can any thing keep him alive, and make him well, but the comforts and cordials of Almighty God, Ezek. 33:10,11. Wherefore with such an one God will dwell, to revive the heart, to revive the spirit: "To revive the spirit of the humble, and to revive the heart of the contrite ones."

God gives relief, but it is to comfort them that are cast down, 2 Cor. 7:6. And such are the broken-hearted: as for them that are whole, they need not the physician, Mt. 9:12. They are the broken in spirit that stand in need of relief. Physicians are men of no esteem but with them that feel their sickness; and this is one reason why God is so little accounted of in the world, even because they have not been made sick by the wounding stroke of God. But now when a man is wounded, has his bones broken, or is made sick, and laid at the grave's mouth, who is of that esteem with him as is an able physician? What is so much desired as the relief, comfort, and suitable supplies of the skillful physician in those matters? And thus it is with the broken-hearted; he needs, and God has prepared for him, plenty of the comforts and relief of heaven, to aid and relieve his sinking soul.

Wherefore such a one lieth under all the promises that have support in them, and consolation for men sick and desponding under the sense of sin and the heavy wrath of God: and they, says God, shall be refreshed and revived with them.

The promises are designed for them. He has therefore broken their hearts and has therefore wounded their spirits, that He might make them able to enjoy His reviving relief, that He might minister to them His reviving comforts.

For, indeed, so soon as he is broken, his bowels yearn, and his compassions roll up and down within him, and will not suffer him to endure affliction. Ephraim was one of these; but so soon as God had smitten him, behold his heart, how it works towards Him: "Is Ephraim," saith He, "my dear son?" that is, he is so; "is he a pleasant child?" that is, he is so: "for since I spake against him, I do earnestly remember him still, therefore My bowels are troubled for him; I will surely have mercy upon him, saith the Lord [God]," Jer. 31:18-20. This therefore is another demonstration.

The Son Heals the Broken Heart

Fifthly, As God prefers such a heart, and esteems the man that has it above heaven and earth; as He covets intimacy with such an one, and prepares for him His relief; so when He sent His Son Jesus into the world to be a Saviour, He gave Him a charge to take care of such; yes, that was one of the main reasons He sent Him down from heaven, anointed for His work on earth. "The Spirit of the Lord God is upon Me," saith He, "because [He] hath anointed Me to preach good tidings unto the meek; He hath sent Me to bind up the brokenhearted," etc. Isa. 61:1.

Now that this is meant of Christ, is confirmed by His own lips; for in the days of His flesh He takes this book in His hand, when He was in the synagogue at Nazareth, and reads this very place unto the people, and then tells them, that that very day that Scripture was fulfilled in their ears, Luke 4:16-18.

But see, these are the souls whose welfare is contrived in the heavens: God considered their salvation, their deliverance, their health, before

8

His Son came down. Does this not demonstrate, that a broken-hearted man, that a man of a contrite spirit, is of great esteem with God? I have often wondered at David, that he should give Joab and the men of war a charge, that they take heed that they carry it tenderly to that young rebel Absalom, his son, 2 Sam. 18:5. But that God, the high God, the God against whom we have sinned, should so soon as He has smitten, give His Son a command, a charge, a commission to take care of, to bind up, and heal the broken in heart—this is that which can never be sufficiently admired or wondered at by men or angels.

And as this was His commission, so He acted; as is evidently set forth by the parable of the man who fell among thieves: he went to him, poured into his wounds wine and oil; he bound him up, took him, set him upon his own beast, had him to an inn, gave the host a charge to look well to him, with money in hand, and a promise, at his return, to recompense him in what further he should be expensive while he was under his care. Luke 10:30-35.

Behold, therefore, the care of God which he has for the broken in heart; He has given a charge to Christ His Son, to look well to them, and to bind up and heal their wounds: behold, also, the faithfulness of Christ, who does not hide, but reads this commission as soon as He enters upon His ministry, and also falls into the practical part thereof: "He healeth the broken in heart, and bindeth up their wounds," Psalm 147:3.

And behold, again, into whose care a "broken heart" and "a contrite spirit" has put this poor creature; he is under the care of God, the care and cure of Christ: if a man was sure that his disease had put him under the special care of the king and the queen, yet could he not be sure of life; he might die under their sovereign hands. But here is a man in the favor of God, and under the hand of Christ to be healed; under whose hand, none yet ever died for lack of skill and power in Him to save their life; wherefore this man must live; Christ has in commission not only to bind up his wounds, but to heal them; He has of himself so expounded it in reading His commission: wherefore he that has his heart broken, and that is of a contrite spirit, must not only be taken in hand, but healed; healed of his pain, grief, sorrow, sin, and fears of death and hell fire.

9

Wherefore He adds, that He must give unto such beauty for ashes, the oil of joy for mourning, the garment of praise for the spirit of heaviness, and must comfort all that mourn, Isa. 61:2,3.

This I say, He has in the commission; the broken-hearted are put into His hand, and He has said himself that He will heal him. Hence, He says of that same man, "I have seen his ways and will heal him; I will lead him also, and restore comforts unto him and to his mourners...and I will heal him," Isa. 57:18-19. And this is a fifth demonstration.

Salvation Is for the Broken Heart

Sixthly, As God prefers such a heart, and so esteems the man that has it, as He desires his company, has provided for him His relief, and given a charge to Christ to heal him, so He has promised in conclusion to save him: "[He] saveth such as be of a contrite spirit"; or as the margin has it, that be contrite of spirit, Ps. 34:18.

And this is the conclusion of all; for to save a man is the end of all special mercy: "He saveth such as be of a contrite spirit." To save is to forgive, for without forgiveness of sins we cannot be saved. To save is to preserve one in this miserable world, and to deliver one from all those devils, temptations, snares, and destructions that would, were we not kept, were we not preserved of God, destroy us, body and soul, for ever. To save, is to bring a man, body and soul, to glory, and to give him an eternal mansion-house in heaven, that he may dwell in the presence of this good God, and the Lord Jesus, and to sing to Them the songs of his redemption for ever and ever. This it is to be saved, nor can anything less than this complete the salvation of the sinner. Now, this it is to be the lot of him that is of a broken heart; and the end that God will make with him that is of a contrite spirit, "He saveth such as be contrite of spirit." He saves such: this is excellent.

But do the broken in heart believe this? Can they imagine, that this is to be the end that God has designed them to, and that He intended to make with them in the day in which He began to break their hearts? No, no; they, alas! think quite the contrary! They are afraid that this is but the beginning of death, and a token that they shall never see the face of God with comfort, either in this world or that which is to come. Hence they cry, "Cast me not away from Thy presence;" or, "I am...free among the dead...whom [God] rememberest no more," Ps. 51:11; 83:4,5.

For indeed, the breaking of the heart comes a visible appearance of the wrath of God, and a home-charge from heaven of the guilt of sin to the conscience. This to reason is very dreadful; for it cuts the soul down to the ground. For a wounded spirit none can bear, Prov. 18:14.

It seems also now to this man, that this is but the beginning of hell; but, as it were, the first step down to the pit, when, alas! all these are but the beginnings of love, and that which makes way for life. The Lord kills before He makes alive, He wounds before His hands make whole. Yea, He does the one in order to, or because He would do the other; He wounds, because His purpose is to heal. "He maketh sore, and bindeth up: He woundeth and His hands make whole," Job 5:18; Deut. 32:39; 1 Sam. 2:6.

The Lord kills before He makes alive, He wounds before His hands make whole.

His design, I say, is the salvation of the soul. He scourges, He breaks the heart of every son whom He receives; and woe be to him whose heart God breaks not.

And I have proved what at first I asserted, namely, that a spirit rightly broken, a heart truly contrite, is to God an excellent thing. "A broken and a contrite heart, O God, thou wilt not despise." For thus say I,

1. This is evident, for that it is better than sacrifices; than all sacrifice.

2. The man that has it is of more esteem with God than heaven and earth.

3. God covets such a man for His intimate and house-companion.

4. He reserves for them His relief and spiritual comforts.

5. He has given His Son a charge, a commandment, to take care that the broken-hearted be healed; and He is resolved to heal them.

6. And concluded that the broken-hearted and they that are of a contrite spirit, shall be saved; that is, possessed of the heavens.

Chapter 2

The Character of a Broken Heart

I come now, in order, to show you what a broken heart and what a contrite spirit is. This must be done, because in the discovery of this lies both the comfort of them that have it, and the conviction of them that have it not.

Now that I may do this the better, I must propound, and speak to these four things.

I.   I must show you what an one that heart is that is not broken, that is not contrite.

II.   I must show you how, or with what, the heart is broken, and made contrite.

III.   Show you how, and what it is, when broken, and made contrite. And

IV.   I shall, last of all, give you some signs of a broken and contrite heart.

What a Broken Heart Is Not

The first is: What is a heart that is not broken, that is not contrite.

The Acceptable Sacrifice

1. The heart before it is broken, is hard and stubborn, and obstinate against God and the salvation of the soul, Zech. 7:12; Deut. 2:30; 9:27.

2. It is a heart full of evil imaginations and darkness, Gen. 8:21; Rom. 1:21.

3. It is a heart deceitful and subject to be deceived, especially about the things of an eternal concernment, Isa. 44:20; Deut. 11:16.

4. It is a heart that rather gathereth iniquity and vanity to itself, than any thing that is good for the soul, Ps. 41:6; 94:11.

5. It is an unbelieving heart, and one that will turn away from God to sin, Heb. 3:12; Deut. 17:17.

6. It is a heart not prepared for God, being uncircumcised, nor for the reception of His holy Word, 2 Chron. 12:14; Ps. 78:8; Acts 7:51.

7. It is a heart not single, but double: it will pretend to serve God, but will withal lean to the devil and sin, Ps. 12:2; Ezek. 33:31.

8. It is a heart proud and stout; it loves not to be controlled, though the controller be God himself, Ps. 101:5; Prov. 16:5; Mal. 3.

9. It is a heart that will give place to Satan, but will resist the Holy Ghost, Acts 5:3; 7:51.

10. In a word, it is deceitful above all things and desperately wicked; so wicked, that none can know it, Jer. 17:9.

That the heart before it is broken is such, and worse than I have described it to be, is sufficiently seen by the whole course of the world. Where is the man (whose heart has not been broken, and whose spirit is not contrite) that, according to the Word of God, deals honestly with his own soul?

It is one character of a right heart, that it is sound in God's statutes, and honest, Ps. 119:80; Luke 8:15.

Now, an honest heart will not put off itself, nor be put off with that which will not go for current money with the merchants; I mean, with that which will not go for saving grace at the day of judgment. But, alas! alas! few men, however honest they are to others, have honesty towards themselves; though he is the worst of deceivers who deceives his own soul, as James has it, about the things of his own soul, Jas. 1:22,26. But,

The Word and the Broken Heart

Secondly, I now come to show you with what, and how the heart is broken, and the spirit made contrite.

The instrument with which the heart is broken, and with which the spirit is made contrite, is the Word. "Is not My Word," says God, "like as a fire...and like a hammer that breaketh the rock in pieces?" Jer. 23:29.

The rock in this text, is the heart, which in another place is compared to an adamant,[1] which adamant is harder than flint, Zech. 7:11,12; Ezek. 3:9.

This rock, this adamant, this stony heart, is broken and made contrite by the Word. But it only is so when the Word is as a fire, and as a hammer to break and melt it; and then, and then only, it is as a fire, and a hammer to the heart to break it, when it is managed by the arm of God. No man can break the heart with the Word; no angel can break the heart with the Word; that is, if God forbears to second it by mighty power from heaven. This made Balaam go without a heart rightly broken and truly contrite, though he was rebuked by an angel; and the Pharisees die in their sins, though rebuked for them, and admonished to turn from them, by the Saviour of the world. Wherefore, though the Word is the instrument with which the heart is broken, yet it is not broken with the Word, till that Word is managed by the might and power of God.

This made the prophet Isaiah, after long preaching, cry out, that he had laboured for nought, and in vain: and this made him cry to God, to rend the heavens and come down, that the mountains, or rocky hills, or hearts, might be broken, and melt at His presence, Isa. 49:4; 64:1,2; for he found by experience, that as to this, no effective work could be done, unless the Lord put forth his hand. This also is often intimated in the

---

1.   Adamant—a stone believed to be impenetrably hard.

Scriptures, where it says, when the preachers preached powerfully to the breaking of men's hearts, the Lord worked with them; the hand of the Lord was with them; and the like. Mk. 16:20; Acts 11:21.

Now when the hand of the Lord is with the Word, then it is mighty; it is "mighty through God to the pulling down of strong holds." It is sharp then, as a sword, in the soul and spirit: it sticks like an arrow in the hearts of sinners, causing the people to fall at His foot for mercy. Then it is, as was said afore, as a fire, and as a hammer, to break this rock in pieces. 2 Cor. 10:4; Heb. 4:12; Ps. 110:3.

When the hand of the Lord is with the Word, then it is mighty.

And hence the Word is made mention of under a double consideration:

1.   As it stands by itself.

2.   As attended with power from heaven.

1. As it stands by itself, and is not backed up with saving operation from heaven, it is called the word only, the word barely, or as if it was only the word of man, 1 Thess. 1:5-7; 1 Cor. 4:19,20; 1 Thess. 2:13; because then, it is only as managed by men, who are not able to make it accomplish that work. The Word of God, when in a man's hand only, is like the father's sword in the hand of the sucking child; which sword, though never so well pointed, and though never so sharp on the edges is not *now* able to conquer a foe, and to make an enemy fall and cry out for mercy, because it is but in the hand of the child.

But now, let the same sword be put into the hand of a skillful Father (and God is both skillful and able to manage His Word), and then the sinner, and then the proud helpers too, are both made to stoop and submit themselves: wherefore I say, though the word be the instrument, yet of itself it doth do no saving good to the soul, the heart is not broken, nor the spirit made contrite thereby, it only works death, and leaves men in the chains of their sins, still faster bound over to eternal condemnation. 2 Cor. 2:15,16.

2. But when backed up by mighty power, then the same Word is as the roaring of a lion, as the piercing of a sword, as a burning fire in the

bones, as thunder, and as a hammer that dashes all to pieces. Jer. 25:30; Amos 1:2; 3:8; Acts 2:37; Jer. 20:9; Ps. 29:3-9.

Wherefore, it is to be concluded, that whoever have heard the Word preached, and have not heard the voice of the living God therein, have not as yet had their hearts broken, nor their spirits made contrite for their sins.

And this leads me to the second thing, that, to show how the heart is broken, and the spirit made contrite by the Word; and verily it is when the Word comes home with power. But this is but general: wherefore more particularly.

1. Then the Word works effectually to this purpose, when it finds the sinner and his sin, and shall convince him that it has been discovered. Thus it was with our first father: when he had sinned, he sought to hide himself from God; he gets among the trees of the garden, and there he covers himself; but not thinking himself secure, he covers himself with fig leaves, and now he lies quiet; now God shall not find me, thinks he, nor know what I have done; but lo! by and by, he hears the "voice of the Lord God walking in the garden"; and now, Adam, what do you mean to do? Why, as yet, he cowers and hides his head, and seeks yet to lie undiscovered; but, behold, the Voice cries out, "Adam!" And now he begins to tremble. "Adam, where art thou?" says God; and now Adam is made to answer. But the voice of the Lord God does not leave him here; no, it now begins to search and to inquire after his doings, and to unravel what he had wrapt together and covered, until it made him bare and naked in his own sight before the face of God, Gen. 3:7-11.

Thus therefore does the Word perform, when managed by the arm of God: it finds out, it singles out the sinner, the sinner finds it so; it finds out the sins of the sinner, it unravels his whole life, it strips him, and lays him naked in his own sight, before the face of God; neither can the sinner nor his wickedness be any longer hid and covered; and now the sinner begins to see what he never saw before.

2. Another instance of this, is David, the man of our text; he sins, he sins grossly, he sins and hides it, yea, and seeks to hide it from the

sight of God and man. Well, Nathan is sent to preach a message to him, and that in common, and that in special; in common, by a parable; in special, by a particular application of it to him. While Nathan only preached in common, or in general, David was ignorant and stood as right in his own eyes, as if he had been innocent and as harmless as any man alive; but God had a love for David, and therefore commands His servant Nathan to go home, not only to David's ears, but to David's conscience.

Well, David now must fall: says Nathan, "Thou art the man"; says David, "I have sinned" (2 Sam. 12:1,5,7,13), and then his heart was broken, and his spirit made contrite, as this Psalm and our text doth show.

3. A third instance is that of Saul; he had heard many a sermon, and had become a great professor, yes he was more zealous than many of his equals; but his heart was never broken, nor his spirit ever made contrite, till he heard One preach from heaven, till he heard God, in the Word of God, making inquiry after his sins: "Saul, Saul, why persecutest thou Me?" says Jesus; and then he can stand no longer; for then his heart breaks, then he falls to the ground, then he trembles, then he cries out, "Who art Thou, Lord?" and, "Lord, what wilt Thou have me to do?" Acts 9:4-6.

As I said, The Word works powerfully to this purpose, when it finds the sinner and his sin, and also when it shall convince him that it has found him out. Only I must join here a caution, for every operation of the Word upon the conscience is not saving; nor doth all conviction end in the saving conversion of the sinner. It is then only such an operation of the Word that is intended, when it shows the sinner not only the evil of his ways, but brings the heart sincerely over to God by Christ. And this brings me to the third thing.

What Is a Broken Heart?

Thirdly, I am therefore come to show you how and what the heart is, when broken and made contrite; and this I must do by opening unto you the two chief expressions in the text.

1. What is meant by this word *Broken*.

2. What is meant by this word *Contrite*.

18

The Character of a Broken Heart

1. For this word *Broken*, Tindall renders it a *troubled* heart but I think there is more in it: I take it, therefore, to be a heart *disabled*, as to former actions; even as a man whose bones are broken, is *disabled*, as to his way of running, leaping, wrestling, or anything else, which vainly he tends to do: wherefore that which was called a *broken heart* in the text, he calls his *broken bones*: "Make me," saith he, "to hear joy and gladness; that the bones which Thou hast broken may rejoice," Ps. 51:8. And why is the breaking of the heart compared to the breaking of the bones? When the bones are broken, the outward man is disabled as to what it tends to do: so when the spirit is broken, the inward man is disabled as to what vanity and folly it before delighted in: hence feebleness is joined with this brokenness of heart: "I am feeble," saith he, "and sore broken," Ps. 38:8. I have lost my strength and former vigour, as to vain and sinful courses.

This then it is to have the heart broken; namely, to have it lamed, disabled, and taken off, by sense of God's wrath due to sin, from that course of life it formerly was conversant in; and to show that this work is no fancy, nor done but with great trouble to the soul, it is compared to putting the bones out of joint, the breaking of the bones, the burning of the bones with fire; or as the taking the natural moisture from the bones; the vexing of the bones, etc. Ps. 22:14; Jer. 20:9; Lam. 1:13; Ps. 6:2; Prov. 17:22.

All which are expressions adorned with such similitudes as do undeniably declare, that to sense and feel a broken heart is a grievous thing.

2. What is meant by the word *Contrite*.

A contrite spirit is a penitent one, one sorely grieved, and deeply sorrowful for the sins it has committed against God, and to the damage of the soul; and so it is to be taken in all those places where a contrite spirit is made mention of; as in Ps. 34:18; Isa. 57:15; 66:2.

As a man who gets, by his folly, a broken leg or arm, is very sorry that he was so foolish as to be engaged in such foolish ways of idleness and vanity; so he whose heart is broken with a sense of God's wrath due to his sin, has deep sorrow in his soul, and is greatly repentant, that ever he should be such a fool as, by rebellious doings, to bring himself and his soul to so much sharp affliction. Hence, while others are sporting themselves in vanity, such a one does call his sin his greatest folly: "My wounds stink, and are corrupt," saith David, "because of my foolishness": and again "O God, Thou knowest my foolishness, and my sins are not hid from Thee," Ps. 38:5; 69:5.

Men, whatever they say with their lips, cannot conclude if their hearts still lack breaking, that sin is a foolish thing. Hence it says, "The foolishness of fools is folly," Prov. 14:24. The foolishness of some men is, that they take pleasure in their sins. Their sins are their foolishness, and the folly of their soul lies in the face of this foolishness. But the man whose heart is broken, he is none of these. He cannot be one of these, no more than he who has bones broken can rejoice when he desires to play soccer. Hence to hear others talk foolishly, is to the grief of those whom God has wounded: or, as it is in another place, Their words are like the piercings of a sword, Ps. 69:26; Prov. 12:18.

This, therefore, I take to be the meaning of these two words, *a broken and a contrite spirit.*

Signs of a Broken Heart

Fourthly, and lastly. As to this, I now come more particularly to give you some signs of a broken heart, of a broken and contrite spirit.

1. A broken-hearted man, a broken heart is sensible as intended in the text, is a sensible man; he is brought to the exercise of all the senses of his soul. All others are dead, senseless, and without true feeling or what the broken-hearted man is sensible of.

(1) He *sees* himself to be what others are ignorant of; that is, he sees himself to be not only a sinful man, but a man by nature in the gall and bond of sin. In the gall of sin: it is Peter's expression to Simon, and it is a saying common to all men; for every man, in the state of nature, is in the gall of sin. He was shapen in it, conceived in it; it has also possession of, and by that possession has infected the whole of his soul and body, Ps. 51:5; Acts 8:23.

This he sees, this he understands; not every teacher sees this, because the blessing of a broken heart is not bestowed on every one. David says, "There is no soundness in my flesh." And Solomon suggests, that a plague or running sore is in every heart: but every one perceives not this, Ps. 38:3; 1 Kings 8:38.

He says again, that his wounds stank, and were corrupted; that his sore ran, and ceased not," Ps. 38:5; 77:2.

But these things the brutish man, the man whose heart was never broken, has no understanding of; but the broken-hearted, the man that has a broken spirit, he sees—as the prophet has it—he sees his sickness, he sees his wound: "when Ephraim saw his sickness, and Judah saw his wound," Hos. 5:13. He sees it to his grief, he sees it to his sorrow.

The broken-hearted feels what others have no sense of.

(2) He *feels* what others have no sense of. He *feels* the arrows of the Almighty, and that they stick fast in him. He *feels* how sore and sick, by the smiting of God's hammer upon his heart to break it, his poor soul is made. He *feels* a burden intolerable lying upon his spirit. "Mine iniquities," saith he, "are gone over mine head: as an heavy burden they are too heavy for me." He *feels* also the heavy hand of God upon his soul; a thing unknown to carnal men. Ps. 38:2; Hos. 5:13; Ps. 38:4.

He *feels* pain, being wounded, even such pains as others cannot understand, because they are not broken. "My heart," says David, "is sore pained within me." Why so? Why, "The terrors of death are fallen upon me." The terrors of death cause pain, yea, pain of the highest nature. Hence, that which is here called "pains," is in another place called "pangs," Ps. 55:4; Isa. 21:3.

You know, broken bones occasion pain, strong pain, yes, pain that will make a man or woman "groan...with the groanings of a deadly wounded man," Ezek. 30:24.

Soul-pain is the sorest pain, in comparison to which the pain of the body is a very tolerable thing, Prov. 18:14.

Now, here is soul-pain, here is heart-pain, here we are discoursing of a wounded, of a broken spirit. Wherefore this pain is to be felt to the sinking of the whole man; neither can any support this but God. Here is death in this pain—death for ever, without God's special mercy, this pain will bring the soul to, and this the broken-hearted man doth feel. "The sorrows of death," said David, "compassed me, and the pains of hell got hold upon me: I found trouble and sorrow," Ps. 116:3.

Aye, I'll guarantee you, poor man, that you found trouble and sorrow indeed; for the pains of hell, and sorrows of death, are pains and sorrows the most intolerable. But this the man is acquainted with, that has his heart broken.

(3) As he *sees* and *feels*, so he *hears* that which augments his woe and sorrow. You know, if a man has his bones broken, he does not only *see* and *feel*, but oftentimes also *hears* what increases his grief; as his wound is incurable, and his bone is not rightly set, there is also a danger of gangrene, that he might miss because he wasn't looking for it. These are the voices, the sayings that haunt the house of one that has his bones broken. And a broken-hearted man knows what I mean by this: he hears that which makes his lips quiver, and at the noise of which he seems to feel rottenness enter into his bones. He trembles in himself, and wishes that he may hear joy and gladness, that the bones, the heart, and spirit, which God has broken, may rejoice, Hab. 3:16; Ps. 51:8.

He thinks he hears God say, the devil say, his conscience say, and all good men to whisper among themselves, saying, "There is no help for him in God." Job heard this, David heard this, Heman heard this; and this is a common sound in the ears of the broken-hearted.

(4) The broken-hearted *smell* what others cannot scent. Alas! sin never *smelled* so to any man alive, as it *smells* to the broken-hearted. You know, wounds will stink; but no stink like that of sin, to the broken-hearted man: his own sins stink, and so do the sins of all the world to him. Sin is like decaying flesh, it is of a stinking nature; it has the worst of smells, however some men like it, Ps. 38:5.

22

But none are offended with the scent thereof, but God and the broken-hearted sinner: "My wounds stink, and are corrupt," saith he, "both in God's nostrils, and mine own."

But alas! who smells the stink of sin? None of the carnal world; they, like vultures, seek it, love it, and eat it as the child eats bread. "They eat up the sin of my people," saith God, "and set their heart on their iniquity," Hos. 4:8.

This, I say, they do, because they do not smell the nauseous scent of sin. You know, what is nauseous to the smell cannot be palatable to the taste. The broken-hearted man doth find that sin is nauseous, and therefore cries out, "It stinketh." They also think at times the smell of fire, of fire and brimstone, is upon them, they are so sensible to the wages of sin.

(5) The broken-hearted is also a *tasting* man. Wounds, if sore and full of pains, of great pains, do sometimes alter the taste of a man: they make him think that his meat, his drink, and even his parties have a bitter taste in them. How many times do the poor people of God, the only ones that know what a broken heart doth mean, cry out, that gravel, wormwood, gall, and vinegar, was made their meat, Lam. 3:15,16,19.

This gravel, gall, and wormwood, is the true temporal taste of sin; and God, to make them loathe it for ever, doth feed them with it till their hearts doth ache and break therewith. Wickedness is pleasant of taste to the world: hence it is said, They feed on ashes, they feed on wind, Isa. 44:20; Hos. 12:1. Lusts, or any thing that is vile and refuse, the carnal world think tastes well; as is set out most notably in the parable of the prodigal son: "He would fain have filled his belly," saith our Lord, "with the husks that the swine did eat," Lk. 15:16. But the broken-hearted man has a relish that is true as to these things; though by reason of the anguish of his soul, it also abhors all manner of dainty meat, Job 33:19,20; Ps. 107:17-19.

Thus I have showed you *one* sign of a broken-hearted man: he is a sensible man, he has all the senses of his soul awakened; he can *see, hear, feel, taste, smell,* and that as none but himself can do. I come now to another sign of a broken and contrite man.

23

The Acceptable Sacrifice

A Broken Heart Is Sorrowful

2. And that is, he is a very sorrowful man. Thus, as the other is natural, it is natural to one that is in pain, and that has his bones broken, to be a grieved and sorrowful man. He is none of the jolly ones of the times, nor can he be, for his bones, his heart, his heart is broken.

(1) He is sorry that he feels and finds in himself a depravity of nature. I told you before, he is sensible of it, he sees it, he feels it; and here I say, he is sorry for it. It is this that makes him call himself, wretched man! It is this that makes him loathe and abhor himself; it is this that makes him blush—blush before God, and be ashamed. Rom. 7:24; Job 42:5,6; Ezek. 36:31.

He finds by nature no form nor comeliness in himself; but the more he looks in the glass of the Word, the more unhandsome, the more deformed he perceiveth sin has made him. Not everybody sees this, therefore everybody is not sorry for it: but the broken in heart sees that he is by sin corrupted, marred, full of lewdness and naughtiness; he sees that in him, that is, in his flesh dwells no good thing; and this makes him sorry, yes, it makes him sorry at heart. A man that has his bones broken finds he is spoiled, marred, disabled from doing as he would and should, at which he is grieved and made sorry.

Many are sorry for actual transgressions, because afterwards they bring them to shame before men; but few are sorry for the defects that sin has made in nature, because they see not those defects themselves. A man cannot be sorry for the sinful defects of nature, till he sees they have rendered him contemptible to God; nor is it any thing but a sight of God, that can make him truly see what he is, and so be heartily sorry for being so. Now "mine eyes see thee," said Job; "now I abhor myself." "Woe is me, I am undone," said the prophet, "for mine eyes have seen the Lord, the King." And it was this that made Daniel say, his comeliness in him was turned into corruption; for he had now the vision of the Holy One, Job 42:6; Isa. 6:1-5; Dan. 10:8.

Visions of God break the heart, because by the sight the soul then has of His perfections, it sees its own infinite and unspeakable disproportion, because of the vileness of its nature.

Visions of God break the heart.

Suppose a company of ugly, uncomely, deformed persons lived together in one house, and suppose that they never yet saw any man or woman more than themselves, that were arrayed with the splendours and perfections of nature; these would not be capable of comparing themselves with any but themselves, and consequently would not be affected, and made sorry, for their uncomely, natural defections. But now, bring them out of their cells and holes of darkness, where they have been shut up by themselves, and let them take a view of the splendour and perfections of beauty that are in others, and then, if at all, they will be sorry and dejected at the view of their own defects.

This is the case: men by sin are marred, spoiled, corrupted, depraved, but they dwell by themselves in the dark; they see neither God, nor angel, nor saint, in their excellent nature and beauty; and therefore they are apt to count their own uncomely parts their ornaments, and their glory. But now, let such, as I said, see God, see saints, or the ornaments of the Holy Ghost, and themselves as they are without them, and then they cannot but be affected with, and sorry for, their own deformity. When the Lord Christ put forth but little of His excellency before His servant Peter's face, it raised up the depravity of Peter's nature before him, to his great confusion and shame, and made him cry out to Him in the midst of all his fellows, "Depart from me, for I am a sinful man, O Lord," Luke 5:4-8.

This, therefore, is the cause of a broken heart; even a sight of Divine excellences, and a sense that I am a poor, depraved, spoiled, defiled wretch; and this sight, having broken the heart, begets sorrow in the broken-hearted.

(2) The broken-hearted is a sorrowful man, because he finds his depravity of nature strong in him, to the showing of itself to oppose and

overthrow what his changed mind does prompt him to do. "When I would do good," said Paul, "evil is present with me," Rom. 7:21. Evil is present to oppose, to resist, and make head against the desires of my soul. The man that has his bones broken may have yet a mind to be industriously occupied in a lawful and honest calling, but he finds by experience that an infirmity attends his present condition, that strongly rests his good endeavours; and at this he shakes his head, makes complaints, and with sorrow of heart he sighs and says that he cannot do the thing that he would, Rom. 7:15; Gal. 5:17.

I am weak, I am feeble, I am not only depraved, but by that depravity deprived of ability to put good motions, good intentions and desires into execution, to completeness: Oh, says he, I am ready to halt, my sorrow is continually before me.

You must know, the broken-hearted loves God, loves his soul, loves good, and hates evil. Now, for such an one to find in himself an opposition and continual contradiction to this holy passion, it must needs cause sorrow; "godly sorrow," as the apostle Paul calls it. For such are made sorry after a godly sort. To be sorry because your nature is sin depraved, and that through this depravity you are deprived of ability to do what the Word and your holy mind does prompt you to do—this is to be sorry after a godly sort; for this sorrow works that in you, of which you will never have cause to repent; no, not to eternity, 2 Cor. 7:9-11.

(3) The broken-hearted man is sorry for those breaches that by reason of the depravity of his nature, are made in his life and conversation. And this was the case of the man in our text. The vileness of his nature had broken out to the defiling of his life, and to the making of him at this time base in conversation. This, this was it that did all to break his heart.

He saw in this he had dishonored God, and that cut him: "Against thee, thee only, have I sinned, and done this evil in thy sight," Ps. 51:4. He saw in this he had caused the enemies of God to open their mouths and blaspheme; and this cut him to the heart. This made him cry, "I have sinned against thee, Lord": this made him say, "I will declare mine iniquity, I will be sorry for my sin," Ps. 38:18.

The Character of a Broken Heart

When a man is designed to do a matter, when his heart is set upon it—and the broken-hearted does design to glorify God—an obstruction to that design, the spoiling of this work, makes him sorrowful. Hannah coveted children, but could not have them, and this made her "a woman of a sorrowful spirit," 1 Sam. 1:15.

A broken-hearted man would be well inwardly, and do that which is well outwardly, but he feels, he finds, he sees he is prevented, prevented at least in part. This makes him sorrowful; in this he groans, groans earnestly, being burdened with his imperfection, 2 Cor. 5:1-3.

You know, one with broken bones has imperfections many, and is more sensible of them too (as was said afore), than any other man; and this makes him sorrowful, yes, and makes him conclude that he shall go softly all his days, in the bitterness of his soul, Isa. 38:15.

A Broken Heart Is Humble

3. The man with a broken heart is a very humble man; for true humility is a sign of a broken heart. Hence, brokenness of heart, contrition of spirit, and humbleness of mind, are put together. "To revive the spirit of the humble, and to revive the heart of the contrite ones," Isa. 57:15.

To follow our similitude. Suppose a man while in bodily health, stout and strong, and one that fears and cares for no man; yet let this man have but a leg or an arm broken, and his courage is quelled; he is now beyond being able to intimidate any man, that he is afraid of every little child that does but offer to touch him. Now he will court the most feeble that has aught to do with him, to use him and handle him gently. Now he is become a child in courage, a child in fear, and humbleth himself as a little child.

So it is with that man that is of a broken and contrite spirit. Time was, indeed, he could swagger, even try to intimidate God by himself, saying, "What is the Almighty, that we should serve him? and what profit should we have, if we pray unto him?" Job 21:15; Mal. 3:13,14.

27

But now his heart is broken, God has wrestled with him, and given him a fall, to the breaking of his bones, his heart; and now he crouches, now he cringes, now he begs of God, that He will not only do him good, but do it with tender hands. "Have mercy upon me, O God," said David, "according unto the multitude of Thy tender mercies blot out my transgressions," Ps. 51:1.

He stands, as he sees, not only in need of mercy, but of the tenderest mercies; God has several sorts of mercies, some more rough, some more tender. God can save a man, and yet have him a dreadful way to heaven. This the broken-hearted sees, and this the broken-hearted dreads, therefore pleads for the tenderest sort of mercies; and here we read of His gentle dealing, and that He is very pitiful, and that He deals tenderly with His. But the reason of such expressions no man knows, but he that is broken-hearted, he has his sores, his running sores, his stinking sores. Wherefore he is pained, and therefore covets to be handled tenderly. Thus God has broken the pride of his spirit, and humbled the loftiness of man. And his humility yet appears.

(1) In his thankfulness for natural life. He considers at night when he goes to bed, that like as a lion, so God will tear him to pieces before the morning light, Isa. 38:13.

There is no judgment that has fallen upon others, but he counts of right he should be swallowed up by it. "My flesh trembleth for fear of Thee; and I am afraid of Thy judgments," Ps. 119:120.

But perceiving a day added to this life, and that he in the morning is still on this side hell, he cannot choose but take notice of it, and acknowledge it as a special favor, saying, "God be thanked, for holding my soul in life till now, and for keeping my life back from the destroyer." Compare Job 33:22; and Ps. 56:13; Ps. 86:13.

Man before his heart is broken, counts time as his own, and therefore he spends it lavishingly upon every idle thing. His soul is far from fear, because the rod of God is not upon him; but when he sees himself under the wounding hand of God, or when God like a lion is breaking all his bones, then he humbles himself before Him, and falls at His foot. Now

28

he has learned to count every moment a mercy, and every small morsel a mercy.

(2) Now also, the least hope of mercy for his soul, oh how precious is it! He that tended to make sport of the Gospel, and that valued promises but as stubble, and the words of God but as rotten wood: now, with what an eye he doth look on the promise! Yea, he counteth a peradventure of mercy more rich, more worth than the whole world. Now, as we say, "He is glad to leap at a crust"; now, to be a dog in God's house, is counted better by him than to dwell in the tents of the wicked, Mt. 15:26,27; Lk. 15:17-19.

(3) Now he that tends to look scornfully upon the people of God; yea, that used to scorn to show them a gentle cast of his countenance; now he admires and bows before them, and is ready to lick the dust off their feet; and would count it his greatest, the highest honour, to be as one of the least of them. "Make me as one of thy hired servants," says he, Luke 15:19.

(4) Now he is in his own eyes the greatest fool in nature, for that he sees he has been so mistaken in his ways, and has yet but little if any true knowledge of God. Every one now, says he, has more knowledge of God than I, every one serves him better than I. Ps. 73:21,22; Prov. 30:2,3.

(5) Now, may he be but one, though the least in the kingdom of heaven! Now, may he be but one, though the least in the church on earth! Now, may he be but loved, though the least beloved of saints! How high an account does he set thereon!

(6) Now when he talks with God or men, how does he debase himself before them! If with God, how does he accuse himself, and load himself with the acknowledgments of his own crime, which he committed in the days wherein he was the enemy of God! "Lord," said Paul, that contrite one, "I imprisoned, and beat in every synagogue them that believed on Thee: And when the blood of Thy martyr Stephen was shed, I also was standing by, and consenting unto his death, and kept the raiment of them that slew him," Acts 22:19,20. "And I punished [Thy saints] oft in every

29

synagogue, and compelled them to blaspheme; and being exceeding mad against them, I persecuted them even unto strange cities," Acts 26:11.

Also, when he comes to speak to saints, how does he make himself vile before them! "I am," saith he, "the least of the apostles, that am not meet to be called an apostle; I am less than the least of all saints: I was a blasphemer, I was a persecutor, and injurious," etc. I Cor. 15:9; Eph. 3:8; 1 Tim. 1:13.

What humility, what self-abasing thoughts, does a broken heart produce! When David danced before the ark of God also, how did he discover his nakedness to the disliking of his wife! And when she taunted him for his doings, says he, "It was before the Lord, etc. And I will be yet more vile than thus, and will be base in mine own sight," 2 Sam. 6:20-22.

Oh, the man that is, or that has been kindly broken in his spirit, and that is of a contrite heart, is a lowly, a humble man!

A Broken Heart Is Poor

4. The broken-hearted man is a man that sees himself in spirituals to be poor: therefore as *humble* and *contrite*, so *poor* and *contrite* are put together in the word: "But to this man will I look, even to him that is poor and of a contrite spirit," Isa. 66:2.

And here we still peruse our metaphor. A wounded man, a man with broken bones, concludes his condition to be but poor, very poor. Ask him how he does, and he answers, "Truly neighbour, in a very poor condition." Also you have the spiritual poverty of such as have, or have had their hearts broken, and that have been of contrite spirits, much made mention of in the Word. And they go by two names, to distinguish them from others: they are called *thy* poor, that is, God's poor; they are also called "the poor in spirit," Ps. 72:2; 74:19; Mt. 5:3.

Now, the man that is poor in his own eyes (for of him we now discourse, and the broken-hearted is such an one), is aware of his wants. He knows he cannot help himself, and therefore is forced to be content to live by the charity of others. Thus it is in nature, thus it is in grace.

30

First, The broken-hearted now knows his wants, and he knew it not till now. As he that has a broken bone knew no need of a bone-setter till he knew his bone was broken, his broken bone makes him know it, his pain and anguish make him know it; and thus it is in spirituals. Now he sees that to be poor indeed is to want the sense of the favour of God; for his great pain is a sense of wrath, as has been shown before; and the voice of joy would heal his broken bones, Ps. 51:8.

Two things, he thinks, would make him rich.

1.   A right and title to Jesus Christ and all His benefits.

2.   A saving faith therein. They that are spiritually rich, are rich in him, and in the faith of him, 2 Cor. 8:9; Jam. 2:5.

The first of these gives us a *right* to the kingdom of heaven, and the second yields the soul the *comfort* of it; and the broken-hearted man wants the sense and knowledge of his interest in these. That he knows he wants them is plain, but that he knows he has them is what as yet he wants the attainment of. Hence he says, "The poor and needy seek water, and there is none, and their tongue faileth for thirst." There is none in their view, none in their view of them, Isa. 41:17.

Hence David, when he had his broken heart, felt he wanted washing, he wanted purging, he wanted to be made white: he knew that spiritual riches lay there, but he did not so well perceive God had washed and purged him: yes, he rather was afraid that all was going, that he was in danger of being cast out of God's presence, and that the Spirit of grace would be utterly taken from him. See Ps. 51.

That is the first thing: the broken-hearted is poor, because he knows his lacks.

Secondly, The broken-hearted is poor because he knows he cannot help himself to what he knows he wants. The man that has a broken arm, as he knows it, so he knows of himself he cannot set it. This, therefore, is a second thing that declares a man is poor, otherwise he is not so: for, suppose a man wants never so much, yet, if he can but help himself, if he can furnish himself, if he can support his own want out of what he has,

31

he cannot be a poor man: yes, the more he wants, the greater his riches, if he can supply his own wants out of his own purse.

He, then, is the poor man, that knows his spiritual want, and also knows he cannot supply or help himself.

But this the broken-hearted knows; therefore he, in his own eyes, is the only poor man. True, he may have something of his own, but that will not supply his want, and therefore he is a poor man still. I have sacrifices, says David, but thou doest not desire them, therefore my poverty remains, Ps. 51:16.

Lead is not gold, lead is not current money with the merchant: there is none has spiritual gold to sell, but Christ, Rev. 3:18.

What can a man do to gain Christ, to gain faith or love? Yes, had he never so much of his own carnal excellences, no not one penny of it will go for pay in that market where grace is to be had. "If a man would give all the substance of his house for love, it would utterly be contemned," Song 8:7.

This the broken-hearted man perceives, and, therefore, he sees himself to be spiritually poor. True, he has a broken heart, and that is of great esteem with God; but that is not nature's goodness, that is a gift, a work of God, that is "the sacrifices of God." Besides, a man cannot remain content and at rest with that; for that, in the nature of it, does but show him he is poor, and that his wants are such as himself cannot supply. Besides, there is but little ease in a broken heart.

Thirdly, The broken-hearted man is poor, and sees it; because he finds he is now disabled to live any way else but by begging.

This David betook himself to, though he was a king; for he knew, as to his soul's health, he could live no way else. "This poor man cried," saith he, "and the Lord heard him, and saved him out of all his troubles," Ps. 34:6. And this leads me to the fifth sign.

A Broken Heart Will Cry

5. Another sign of a broken heart is a crying, a crying out. Pain, you know, will make one cry: go to them that have upon them the anguish of broken bones, and see if they do not cry; anguish makes them cry.

This is that which quickly follows, if once thy heart be broken, and your spirit indeed made contrite.

First, I say, anguish will make you cry. "Trouble and anguish," said David, "have taken hold on me," Ps. 119:143. Anguish, you know, doth naturally provoke to crying: now, as a broken bone has anguish, a broken heart has anguish; hence the pains of one that has a broken heart are compared to the pangs of a woman in travail, John 16:20-22.

1. Anguish will make one cry alone, cry to oneself; and this is called a bemoaning of oneself. "I have surely heard Ephraim bemoaning himself," said God, Jer. 31:18.

That is, being at present under the breaking, chastising hand of God: "Thou has chastised me," saith he, "and I was chastised, as a bullock unaccustomed to the yoke," Jer. 31:18. This is his meaning also who said, "I mourn in my complaint, and make a noise;" and why? Why? "my heart is pained sore within me," Ps. 55:2-4.

This is a self-moaning, a bemoaning themselves in secret and retired places.

You know it is common with them who are distressed with anguish, though all alone, to cry out to themselves of their present pains; say, O my leg! O my arm! O my bowels! or, as the son of the Shunammite, "My head, my head!" 2 Kings 4:19. O the groans, the sighs, the cries, that the broken-hearted have when by themselves, or alone. O, say they, My sins, my sins! my soul, my soul! How am I laden with guilt! how am I surrounded with fear! O this hard, this desperate, this unbelieving heart! O how sin defileth my will, my mind, my conscience! "I am afflicted and ready to die," Ps. 88:15.

Could some of you carnal people but get behind the chamber door to hear Ephraim when he is at the work of self-bemoaning, it would make you stand amazed to hear him bewail that sin in himself in which you take delight, and to hear him bemoan his misspending of time, while you spend all in pursuing your filthy lusts, and to hear him offended with his heart because it will not better comply with God's holy will, while you are afraid of His Word and ways, and never think yourselves better than when farthest off from God. The unruliness of the passions, the lusts of the broken-hearted, make them often get into a corner, and thus bemoan themselves.

Secondly, As they cry out in a bemoaning manner of and to themselves, so they have their outcries of and against themselves to others; as she said in another case, "Behold, and see if there be any sorrow like unto my sorrow," Lam. 1:12.

Oh, the bitter cries and complaints that the broken-hearted have, and make to one another! still every one imagining that his own wounds are deepest, and his own sores fullest of anguish, and hardest to be cured. Say then, "If our transgressions...be upon us, and we pine away in them, how should we then live?" Ezek. 33:10.

Once, being at an honest woman's house, I, after some pause asked her how she was doing. She said, "Very badly." I asked her if she was sick. She answered, "No." "What then?" said I, "are any of your children ill?" She told me, "No." "What," said I, "is your husband amiss, or do you go back in the world?" "No, no," said she, "but I am afraid I shall not be saved"; and brake out with a heavy heart, saying, "Ah, good-man Bunyan, Christ and a pitcher! If I had Christ, though I went and begged my bread with a pitcher, it would be better with me than I think it is now."

This woman had her heart broken; this woman wanted Christ; this woman was concerned for her soul. There are but few women, rich women, that count Christ and a pitcher better than the world, their pride, and pleasures. This woman's cries are worthy to be recorded: it was a cry that carried in it not only a sense of the want, but also of the worth of Christ. This cry, "Christ and a pitcher," made a melodious noise in the ears of the very angels.

But, I say, few women cry out thus; few women are so in love with their own eternal salvation as to be willing to part with all their lusts and vanities for Jesus Christ and a pitcher. Good Jacob also was thus: If the Lord, said he, will give me bread to eat and raiment to put on, then He shall be my God: yea, he vowed it should be so. "And Jacob vowed a vow, saying, If God will be with me, and keep me in this way that I go, and will give me bread to eat, and raiment to put on, so that I come again to my father's house in peace; then shall the Lord be my God," Gen. 28:20,21.

3. As they bemoan themselves, and make their complaints to one and another, so they cry to God. "O God," said Heman, "I have cried day and night before thee." But when? Why, when his soul was full of trouble, and his life drew near to the grave (Ps. 88:1-3); or, as it says in another place, "Out of the deep, out of the belly of hell, cried I": by such words, expressing what painful condition they were in when they cried, Ps. 130:1; Jonah 2:2.

See how God himself words it: My pleasant portion, says He, is become a desolate wilderness; "and being desolate, it mourneth unto Me," Jer. 12:10-11.

And this also is natural to those whose heart is broken. Where does the child go when it gets in trouble but to its father; to its mother? Where doth it lay its head but in their laps? Into whose bosom doth it pour out its complaint more especially, but into the bosom of a father, of a mother? because there are bowels, there is pity, there is relief and succour. And thus it is with them whose bones, whose heart is broken: it is natural to them, they must cry, they cannot but cry to him. "Lord, heal me," said David, "for my bones are vexed"; Lord, heal me, for my soul is vexed, Ps. 6:1-3.

> *A broken heart trembles at God's Word.*

He that cannot cry, feels no pain, sees no want, fears no danger, or else is dead.

6. Another sign of a broken heart, and of a contrite spirit, is, it trembleth at God's Word—"to him that is poor, and of a contrite spirit, and trembleth at My Word," Isa. 66:2.

The Acceptable Sacrifice

The Word of God is an awful word to a broken-hearted man. Solomon says, "The fear of a king is as the roaring of a lion," Prov. 20:2; and if so, what is the word of God? for, by the wrath and fear is meant the authoritative word of a King.

We have a proverb, "The burnt child dreads the fire, the whipped child fears the rod"; even so the broken-hearted fears the Word of God. Hence you have a mark set upon them that tremble at God's Word: to wit, they are they that keep among the godly; they are they that keep within compass; they are they that are more able to mourn and to stand in the gap when God is angry, and to turn away His wrath from a people.

It is a sign the Word of God has had place, and worked powerfully, when the heart trembles at it, is afraid, and stands in awe of it. When Joseph's mistress tempted him to lie with her, he was afraid of the Word of God: "How then can I do this great wickedness," said he, "and sin against God?" Gen. 39:7-9. He stood in awe of God's Word, durst not do it, because he kept in remembrance what a dreadful thing it was to rebel against God's Word. When old Eli heard that the ark was taken, his very heart trembled within him; for he read, by that sad loss, that God was angry with Israel, and he knew that the anger of God was a great and terrible thing, 1 Sam. 4:13. When Samuel went to Bethlehem, the elders of the town trembled, for they feared that he came to them with some sad message from God, and they had had experience of the dread of such things before, 1 Sam. 16:1-4.

When Ezra would have a mourning in Israel for the sins of the land, he sent, "Then were assembled unto me every one that trembled at the words of the God of Israel, because of the transgression of those that had been carried away," Ezra 9:4.

There are, I say, a sort of people that tremble at the words of God, and that are afraid of doing aught that is contrary to them; but they are only such with whose souls and spirits the Word has had to do: for the rest they are resolved to go on their course, let God say what he will. "As for the word," said rebellious Israel to Jeremiah, "that thou hast spoken unto us in the name of the Lord, we will not harken unto thee. But we will certainly do whatsoever thing goeth forth out of our own mouth," Jer. 44:16,17. But do you think that these people did ever feel the power and majesty of the Word of God to break their hearts? No verily; had that been so, they would have trembled at the words of God; they would have been afraid of the words of God. God may command some people what He will, they will do what they list. What care they for God? What care they for His Word? Neither threats nor promises, neither punishments nor favours, will make them obedient to the Word of God; and all because they have not felt the power of it, their hearts have not been broken with it. When King Josias did but read in God's book what punishment God had threatened against rebellious Israel, though he himself was a holy and good man, he humbled himself, he rent his clothes, and wept before the Lord, and was afraid of the judgment threatened, 2 Kings 12; 2 Chron. 34: for he knew what a dreadful thing the Word of God is. Some men, as I said before, dare do anything, let the Word of God be ever so much against it; but they that tremble at the Word dare not do so. No, they must make the Word their rule for all they do; they must go to the holy Bible, and there inquire what may or may not be done: for they tremble at the Word.

This, then, is another sign, a true sign, that the heart has been broken, namely, when the heart is made afraid of and trembleth at the Word, Acts 9:4-6; 16:29-31.

Trembling at the Word is caused by a belief of what is deserved and threatened, and of what will come if not prevented by repentance; and, therefore, the heart melts and breaks before the Lord.

Chapter 3

The Reason for a Broken Heart

I come, in the next place, to speak to this question.

But what necessity is there that the heart must be broken? Cannot a man be saved unless his heart be broken?

I answer, avoiding secret things, which only belong to God, there is a necessity of breaking the heart in order to bring salvation, because a man will not sincerely comply with the means lending thereto until his heart is broken. For,

First, Man, take him as he comes into the world, as to spirituals, as to evangelical things, in which mainly lies man's eternal felicity, and there he is as one dead, and so stupefied, and wholly selfish, as if unconcerned with it; nor can any call nor admonition that has not a heart-breaking power attending of it, bring him to a due consideration of his present state, and so unto an effectual desire to be saved.

Many ways God has manifested this:

1. He has threatened men with temporal judgments; yes, sent such judgments upon them once and again, over and over, but they will not do. What, says He, "I also have given you cleanness of teeth in all your

cities...I have withholden the rain from you...I have smitten you with blasting and mildew...I have sent among you the pestilence...I have overthrown some of you, as God overthrew Sodom and Gomorrah...yet have ye not returned unto Me, saith the Lord," Amos 4:6-11.

See here! here is judgment upon judgment, stroke after stroke, punishment after punishment; but all will not do unless the heart is broken! Another prophet seems to say, that such things, instead of converting the soul, set it further off, if heart-breaking work attend not such strokes. "Why should ye be stricken any more?" says He: "ye will revolt more and more," Isa. 1:5.

Man's heart is fenced, it is grown gross, there is a skin that, like a coat-of-mail[1] has wrapped it up, and enclosed it on every side. This skin, this coat-of-mail, unless it be cut off and taken away, the heart remains untouched, whole; and so as unconcerned, whatever judgments of afflictions light upon the body, Mt. 13:15; Acts 28:27.

This which I call the coat-of-mail, the *sense* of the heart, has two great names in Scripture: it is called the foreskin of the heart, and the armour in which the devil trusteth, Deut. 10:16; Luke 11:22.

Because these shield and fence the heart from all Gospel doctrine and from all legal punishments, nothing can come at it till these are removed: therefore, in order unto conversion, the heart is said to be circumcised; that is, this foreskin is taken away, and this coat-of-mail is spoiled. "[I] will circumcise thine heart," said He, "to love the Lord thy God with all thine heart" (and then the devil's goods are spoiled), "that thou mayest live," Deut. 30:6; Luke 11:22.

And now the heart lies open, now the Word will prick, cut, and pierce it; and it being cut, pricked, and pierced, it bleeds, it faints, it falls and dies at the foot of God, unless it is supported by the grace and love of God in Jesus Christ.

Conversion, you know, begins at the heart; but if the heart be so secured by sin and Satan, as I have said, all judgments are, while that is so, in vain. Hence Moses, after he had made a long relation of mercy and

---

1.   Coat-of-mail—a garment of metal scabs or rings that is worn as an armor.

judgment unto the children of Israel, suggests that yet the great thing was wanting to them, and that thing was "an heart to perceive, and eyes to see, and ears to hear unto this day," Deut. 29:4.

Their hearts were as yet not touched to the quick, were not awakened and wounded by the holy Word of God, and made to tremble at its truth and terror.

But I say, before the heart be touched, pricked, made to smart, etc., how can it be thought, be the danger ever so great, that it should repent, bow, and break at the foot of God, and supplicate there for mercy? And yet thus it must do; for thus God has ordained, and thus God has appointed it: nor can men be saved without it.

But I say, Can a man spiritually dead—a stupid man, whose heart is past feeling—do this, before he has his dead and stupid heart awakened to see and feel its state and misery without it? But,

Secondly, Man, take him as he comes into the world, and however wise he is in worldly and temporal things, he is yet a fool as to that which is spiritual and heavenly. Hence he says, "The natural man receiveth not the things that are of the Spirit of God: for they are foolishness unto him" (because he is indeed a fool to them): "neither," says the text, "can he know them, because they are spiritually discerned," 1 Cor. 2:14.

But how, now, must this fool be made wise? Why, wisdom must be put into his heart, Job 38:36.

Now, none can put in there but God; and how does He put it there but by making room there for it, by taking away the thing which hinders, which is that folly and madness which naturally dwells there? But how does He take that away but by a severe chastising of his soul for it, until He has made him weary of it? The whip and stripes are provided for the natural fool, and so it is for him that is spiritually so, Prov. 19:29.

Solomon intimates that it is a hard thing to make a fool become wise: "Though thou shouldest bray a fool in a mortar among wheat with a pestle,[2] yet will not his foolishness depart from him," Prov. 27:22.

---

2.   Pestle—an implement for grinding substances in a mortar.

The Acceptable Sacrifice

By this it appears that it is a hard thing to make a fool a wise man. To pound one in a mortar is a dreadful thing—to pound one there with a hammer! and yet it seems a whip, a mortar, and a hammer is the way. And if this is the way to make one wise in this world, and if all this will hardly do, how much the fool that is so in spirituals be whipped, and beaten, and striped before he is made wise therein? Yes, his heart must be put into God's mortar, and must be beaten, and pounded there with the hammer of the law, before it loves to hearken unto heavenly things. It is a great word in Jeremiah, "Through deceit," that is, folly, "they refuse to know me, saith the Lord." And what follows? Why, "Therefore thus saith the Lord of hosts, Behold, I will melt them, and try them," that is, with fire; "for how shall I do for the daughter of My people?" Jer. 9:6,7.

I will melt them; I will put them into My furnace, and there will I try them, and there I will make them know Me, saith the Lord. When David was under spiritual chastisement for his sin, and had his heart under the breaking hand of God, then he said, God should make him know wisdom, Ps. 51:6.

Now he was in the mortar, now he was in the furnace, now he was bruised and melted; yes, now his bones and his heart were breaking, and now his folly was departing. Now, says he, "thou shalt make me to know wisdom." If I know anything of the way of God with us fools, there is nothing else will make us wise men; yes, a thousand breakings will not make us so wise as we should be.

We say, Wisdom is not good till it is bought; and he that buys it according to the intention of that proverb, usually smarts for it. The fool is wise in his own conceit; wherefore there is a double difficulty attends him before he can be wise indeed: not only his folly, but his wisdom must be removed from him; and how shall that be but a ripping up of his heart by some sore conviction that may show him plainly that his wisdom is his folly, and that which will undo him. A fool loves his folly as a treasure and he is in love with it. Now, then, it must be a great thing that must make a fool forsake his folly. The foolish will not weigh, nor consider, compare wisdom with their folly. Folly is joy to him that is destitute of wisdom: "As a dog returneth to his vomit, so a fool returneth to his folly";

so loath are they, when driven from it, to let it depart from them, Prov. 15:21; 26:11.

Wherefore, there must be a great deal to make a man a Christian; for, as to that, every man is a fool; yes, the greatest fool, the most unconcerned fool, the most self-willed fool of all fools; yea, one that will not be turned from his folly but by the breaking of his heart. David was one of these fools; Manasseh was one of these fools; Saul, otherwise called Paul, was one of these fools; and so was I, and that the biggest of all.

Thirdly, Man, take him as he comes into the world, and he is not only a dead man and a fool, but a proud man also. Pride is one of those sins that first showeth itself to children; yes, and it grows up with them, and mixeth itself with all they do: but it lies most hid, most deep in man as to his soul concerns; for the nature of sin, as sin, is not only to be vile, but to hide its vileness from the soul. Hence, many think they do well when they sin: Jonah thought he did well to be angry with God; the Pharisees thought they did well when they said Christ had a devil; and Paul thought surely he should do many things against or contrary to the name of Jesus; which he also did with great madness, Jonah 4:9; John 8:48; Acts 26:9,10.

And thus sin puffs up men with pride, and a conceit of themselves that they are a thousand times better than they are: hence they think they are the children of God when they are the children of the devil, and that they are something as to Christianity when they neither are such, nor know what it is that they must have to make them such, John 8:41-44; Gal. 6:3.

Now, whence flows this but from pride and a self-conceit of themselves, and that their state is good for another world, when they are yet in their sins, and under the curse of God: yea, and this pride is so strong and high, and yet so hid in them, that all the ministers in the world cannot persuade them that this is pride, not grace, in which they are so confident.

Hence they slight all reproofs, rebukes, threatenings, or admonitions that are pressed upon them, to prevail with them to take heed that they

43

be not herein deceived. "Hear ye," saith the prophet, "and give ear; be not proud, for the Lord hath spoken," Jer. 13:15, "and if ye will not hear it, my soul shall weep in secret for your pride," verse 17. And what was the conclusion? Why, all the proud men stood out still, and maintained their resistance of God and His holy prophet, Jer. 43:2.

Nor is there any thing that will prevail with these, to the saving of their souls, until their hearts are broken. David, after he had defiled Bathsheba and slain her husband, yet boasted himself in his justice and holiness, and would by all means have the man put to death that had but taken the poor man's lamb (2 Sam. 12:1-6), when, alas! poor soul, himself was the great transgressor. But would he believe it? No, no; he stood upon the vindicating of himself to be a just doer; nor would he be made to fall until Nathan, by authority from God, did tell him that he was the man whom himself had condemned. "Thou art the man," said he; at which word his conscience was awakened, his heart wounded, and so his soul made to fall under the burden of his guilt at the feet of the God of heaven for mercy, verse 7-13.

Ah! pride, pride, thou art that which holds many a man in the chains of his sins: thou art it, thou cursed self-conceit, that keepest them from believing that their state is damnable. "The wicked, through the pride of his countenance, will not seek after God," Ps. 10:4; and if there is so much in the pride of his countenance, what is there, think you, in the pride of his heart?

Therefore Job says, "It is to hide pride from man," and to save his soul from hell, "that God chasteneth him with pain upon his bed, until the multitude of his bones stick out, and until his life draws nigh to the destroyer," Job 33:17-22.

It is a hard thing to take a man off of his pride, and make him, instead of trusting *in* and boasting *of* his goodness, wisdom, honesty, and the like, to see himself a sinner, a fool, yea, a man that is cruel as to his own immortal soul.

Pride of heart has a power in it, and is therefore compared to an iron sinew and an iron chain, by which they are made stout, and with which they are held in that stoutness, to oppose the Lord and drive His Word from their hearts, Lev. 26:19; Ps. 73:6.

This was the sin of devils, and it is the sin of man, and the sin, I say, from which no man can be delivered until his heart is broken; and then his pride is spoiled, then he will be glad to yield.

If a man be proud of his strength or manhood, a broken leg will bruise him; and if a man be proud of his goodness, a broken heart will bruise him; because, as has been said, a broken heart comes by the discovery and charge of sin and by the power of God upon the conscience.

Fourthly, Man, take him as he comes into the world, and he is not only a dead man and a fool, and proud, but also self-willed and headstrong, 2 Pet. 2:10.

A stubborn clumsy creature is man before his heart is broken. So they are often called rebels, rebellious, and disobedient: They will only do what they list. "All day long," says God, "I have stretched forth My hands unto a disobedient and gainsaying people," Rom. 10:21.

And again, they are compared to a self-willed or headstrong horse, that will in spite of his rider rush into the battle. "Every one," says God, "turned to his course, as the horse rusheth into the battle," Jer. 8:6.

They say, "with our tongue will we prevail; our lips are our own: who is lord over us?" Ps. 12:4.

They are said to stop their ear, to pull away their shoulder, to shut their eyes, and harden their hearts against the words of God, and to "[contemn] the counsel of the Most High," Zech. 7:11,12; Ps. 107:11.

They are fitly compared to the rebellious son, who would not be ruled by his parents; or to the prodigal, who would have all his own hand, and remove himself far away from father and father's house, Deut. 21:20; Luke 15:11-13.

Now for such creatures nothing will do but violence. The stubborn son must be stoned till he dies, and the prodigal must be starved till nothing is left; nothing else, I say, will do. Their self-willed, stubborn heart will not comply with the will of God before it is broken, Deut. 21:21; Luke 15:14-17.

These are they that are called the "stouthearted"; these are said to be "far from righteousness," and so will remain until their hearts are broken; for so they must be made to know themselves, Isa. 46:12.

Fifthly, Man, as he comes into the world, is not only a dead man, a fool, proud and self-willed; but also a fearless creature. "There is," saith the text, "no fear of God before their eyes," Rom. 3:18.

No fear of God. There is a fear of man and fear of losing his favor, his love, his good will, his help and his friendship. This is seen every where; how does the poor fear the rich, the weak fear the strong; and those that are threatened, fear them that threaten! But when it comes to God, why do none fear Him. By nature, none reverence Him; they neither fear His frowns, nor seek His favor, nor inquire how they may escape His revenging hand that is lifted up against their sins and their souls because of sin. Little things they fear like the losing of them, but the soul they are not afraid to lose: "[They] fear not Me, saith the Lord," Mal. 3:5.

How many times are some men reminded of death, by sickness upon themselves, by graves, by the death of others?

How many times are they reminded of hell, by reading the Word, by lashes of conscience, and by some that go roaring in despair out of this world?

How many times are they reminded of the day of judgment? As,

1. By God's binding the fallen angels over to judgment, 2 Pet. 2:4; Jude 6.

2. By the drowning of the old world, 2 Pet. 3:5.

3. By the burning of Sodom and Gomorrah with fire from heaven, 2 Pet. 2:6; Jude 7.

4. By appointing a day, Acts 17:29-31.

5. By appointing a Judge, Acts 10:40-42.

6. By preserving their crimes in records, Isaiah 30:8; Rev. 20:12.

7. By appointing and preparing of witnesses, Rom. 2:15.

8. And by promising and threatening and resolving to call the whole world to His bar, there to be judged for all they have done and said, and for every secret thing, Mt. 12:36; 25:31-33; Eccles. 11:9; 12:14.

And yet they do not fear God. Alas! they don't believe these things: these things, to carnal men, are like Lot's preaching to his sons and daughters that were in Sodom; when he told them that God would destroy that place, he seemed unto them as one that mocked; and his words to them were as idle tales, Gen. 19:14.

Fearless men are not won by words; blows, wounds, and killings are the things that must bring them under fear. How many fits of struggle did Israel have with God in the wilderness? how many times did they declare that there they did not fear Him? And, observe, how they were seldom, if ever, brought to fear and dread of his glorious name unless he humbled them with a round with death and the grave. Nothing, nothing but a severe hand will make the *Fearless men are not won by words.* fearless fear: God is moved to act this way with sinners when He would save their souls, even to bring them and lay them at the mouth and within sight of hell and everlasting damnation, and there also charge them with sin and guilt, to the breaking of their hearts, before they will fear His name.

Sixthly, Man as he comes into the world, is not only a dead man, a fool, proud, self-willed, and fearless, but he is a false believer concerning God. Let God report of himself never so plainly, man, by nature, will not believe this report of Him: no; they are become vain in their imaginations, and their foolish heart is darkened. Therefore they turn the glory of God, which is His truth, into a lie, Rom. 1:21-25.

1. God says He sees; they say He sees not. God says He knows: They say He does not know. God says none is like to himself; yet they say He is altogether like to them. God says none shall keep His door for nought; they say it is in vain and to no profit to serve Him. He says He will do good: they say He will neither do good nor evil, Job 22:13,14; Ps. 50:21; Job 21:14,15; Mal. 3:14; Zeph. 1:12.

In this way they falsely believe concerning God: yes, as to the word of His grace and the revelation of His mercy in Christ, by their practice (for a wicked man speaketh with his feet, Prov. 6:13). They say that is a stark lie, and not to be trusted to, 1 John 5:10.

Now, what shall God do to save these men? If He hides himself, and conceals His glory, they perish. If He sends to them His messengers, and forbears to come to them himself, they perish. If He comes to them, and seeks to work upon them by His Word, they perish. If He works on them, but not effectually, they perish. If He works effectually, He must break their hearts, and make them, as men wounded to death, fall at His feet for mercy, or there can be no good done on them: they will not rightly believe until He delivers them out of their misbelief, and makes them to know, by the breaking of their bones for their false faith, that He is, and will be, what He has said of himself in His holy Word. The heart, therefore, must be broken before the man can come to good.

The heart, therefore, must be broken before the man can come to good.

Seventhly, Man, as he comes into the world, is not only a dead man, a fool, proud, self-willed, fearless, and a false believer, but a great lover of sin: he is captivated, ravished, drowned in the delights of it. In this way they are said to love sin, delight in lies, to take pleasure in iniquity, and in them that do it. They delight themselves in their own deceivings, and glory in their shame, John 3:19; Ps. 62:4; Rom. 1:32; 2 Pet. 2:13; Phil. 3:19.

This is the behavior of man by nature, for sin is mixed with, and has the mastery of all the powers of his soul. They are said to be captives to it, and to be led captive into the pleasures of it, at the will of the devil, 2 Tim. 2:26.

And, you know, it is not an easy thing to break love, or to take the affections off of that object on which they are so deeply set, in which they are so deeply rooted as man's heart is in his sins. Alas! how many are there who ogle contempt on all the blessings of heaven, and who trample upon all the threatenings of God. They take lightly all the flames of hell, whenever they are preached as motives to depart from sinful pleasures.

They are so fixed and so mad about these beastly idols: They shall attempt to stop their course in this their way as the one who attempts to prevent the raging waves of the sea from their course when driven by the mighty winds.

When men begin to listen and when reason and conscience shall begin to hear the preacher or a judgment shall begin to hunt for iniquity, how many tricks, evasions, excuses, objections, delays, and hiding-holes will they make, invent, and find to hide. In this way they preserve their sweet sins with themselves and their souls continue to delight in them, to their own eternal perdition. Hence they endeavor to stifle conscience, to choke convictions, to forget God, to make themselves atheists, to contradict preachers that are plain and honest, and to draw to themselves others who are like themselves. They speak unto them smooth things, and prophesy deceits: yes, in this way they tell such preachers, "Get ye out of the way; turn aside out of the path; cause the Holy One of Israel to cease from before us." Isa. 30:8-11.

Soon conscience and guilt shall, like bloodhounds, find them out of their secret places, and roar against them for their wicked lives. Then they will flatter, cog, deceive, and lie against their souls, promising to mend, to turn, to repent, to do better shortly. They will do all of this to throw aside convictions and disturbances in their wicked ways, so that they may still pursue their lusts, their pleasures, and sinful delights in quiet and without control.

I have known some that have been made to roar like bears, to yell like dragons, and to howl like dogs, by reason of the weight of guilt and the lashes of hell upon their conscience for their evil deeds, who have, so soon as their present torments and fears were gone, returned again with "the dog to his vomit," or as "the sow that was washed to her wallowing in the mire," Hos. 7:14; 2 Pet. 2:20-22.

Some have been made to taste of the good word of God, of the joy of heaven, and of the powers of the world to come, and yet could not by any one, nay, by all of these, be made to break their league for ever with their lusts and sins, Heb. 6:1-5; Luke 8:13; John 5:33-35.

O Lord, "what is man, that Thou art mindful of him?" wherein is he to be accounted of? He has sinned against You; he loves his sins more than You: he is a lover of pleasure more than he is a lover of God.

But, now, how shall this man be reclaimed from this sin? how shall he be brought, wrought, and taken out of love with it? Doubtless, it can be by no other means, by what we can see in the Word. It is only by the wounding, breaking, and disabling of the heart that loves it, and by that means making it a plague and gall unto it. Sin may be made an affliction, and as gall and wormwood to them that love it. But the making of it is so bitter a thing to such a man as will not be done but by great and sore means. I remember we had in our town, some time since, a little girl that loved to eat the heads of foul tobacco-pipes, and neither rod nor good words could change her and make her leave them. So her father took advice of a doctor, to wean her from them, and it was this: "Take," he said, "a great many of the foulest tobacco-pipe heads you can get, and boil them in milk, and make a mixture of that milk, and make your daughter drink it all." He did so, and gave it to the girl and made her drink it all. She became so irksome and nauseous to her stomach, and made her so sick, that she was never to mess with tobacco-pipe heads any more, and so was cured of that disease.

Thou lovest thy sin, and neither rod nor good words will as yet reclaim thee. Well, take heed, if you will not be reclaimed, God will make thee a mixed drink which shall be so bitter to thy soul, so irksome to thy taste, so loathsome to thy mind, and so afflicting to thy heart, that it shall break it with sickness and grief, till it be loathsome to thee. I say, thus

50

He will do if He loves you. If not, He will let you take your course, and go on with your tobacco-pipe heads.

The children of Israel will have flesh, must have flesh. They weep, cry, and murmur because they have not flesh: the bread of heaven, that is but light and sorry stuff in their esteem, Num. 11:4-6. Moses goes and tells God how the people despised His heavenly bread, and how they longed, lusted, and desired to be fed with flesh. Well, says God, they shall have flesh, they shall have their fill of flesh. I will feed them with it. They shall have to the full, and that not for a day, or two days, or five days, neither ten days nor twenty days, but even a whole month, until it comes out at their nostrils, and it be loathsome unto them, because they have despised the Lord, Num. 11:11-20.

He knows how to make something despised to you on which you set your evil heart. He will do so if He loves thee. Or else, as I have said, He will not make you sick by smiting you, nor punish you for, or when you commit whoredom, but will let you alone till the judgment day, and call you to a reckoning for all your sins then.

Eighthly, Man, as he comes into the world, is not only a dead man, a fool, proud, self-willed, fearless, a false believer, and a lover of sin, but a wild man. He is of the wild olive tree, of that which is wild by nature, Rom. 11:17,24.

So in another place, man by nature is compared to an ass, to a wild ass; for vain or empty man would be wise, though man be born as a wild ass's colt, Job 11:12.

Isaac was a figure of Christ, and also of all converted men, Gal. 4:28. Ishmael was a figure of man by nature; and the Holy Ghost, as to that, said of him, "And he will be a wild man," Gen. 16:12. This man, I say, was a figure of all carnal men in their wilderness, or estrangedness from God. It is said of the prodigal at his conversion, that he came to himself then, implying that he was mad, wild, or out of his wits before, Luke 15:17.

I know there is a difference sometimes between one's being wild and mad. Yet, sometimes, wildness arrives to that degree as to give one the

51

sense of being mad, and it is always true in spiritual things; namely, that he that is wild as to God is mad, or beside himself, and so not capable, before he is tamed, of minding his own eternal good as he should.

There are these several things that are tokens of one wild or mad, and they all meet in a carnal man.

1. A wild or mad man gives no heed to good counsel. The frenzy of his head shuts even time out, and by its force leads him away from men that are wise and sober; and thus it is with carnal men. Good counsel is to them as pearls that are cast before swine. It is trampled under foot of them, and the man is despised that brings it. "The poor man's wisdom is despised, and his words are not heard," Mt. 7:6; Eccles. 9:16.

2. A wild or mad man left alone, will greatly busy himself all his lifetime to accomplish that which, when it is completed, amounts to nothing. The work, the toil, and the travail of such an one comes to nothing except to declare that he was out of his wits that did it. David, imitating such an one, scribbled upon the gate of the king, as fools do, with chalk. This is all the work of all carnal men in the world, 1 Sam. 21:12,13.

Hence such an one is said to labor for the wind, or for what will amount to no more than if he filled his belly with the east wind, Eccles. 5:16; Job 15:2.

3. A wild or mad man, if you allow him to do any thing and he does it, then he will do it and not according to your bidding, but after the folly of his own wild fancy. Jehu executed the commandment of the Lord, and he did it in his own madness, taking no heed to the commandment of the Lord, 2 Kings 9:20; 10:31.

And so do carnal men do when they meddle with any of God's matters, as hearing, praying, reading, professing. They do all according to their own wild fancy; and they take no heed to do these after the commandment of the Lord.

4. Wild or mad men, if they dress themselves up, as many times they do, then the spirit of their wildness, or frenzy, appears in one of two way in which they do it. Either the things themselves which they make use of

52

for that purpose are very toys and insignificant things, or they are put on after a wild manner, making them ridiculous rather than sober, judicious, or wise. In this way natural men clothe themselves in a way that they would be accepted with God. Would one in his right mind think that to make himself fine or acceptable to men, he would array himself in filthy garments, or by painting his face with dross and dung? And yet this is the best of carnal men when they approach for acceptance into the presence of God, Isa. 54:6; Phil. 3:7,8.

Oh, the wildness, the frenzy, the madness that possess the heart and mind of carnal men! They walk according to the course of this world, according to, or after that spirit which is in truth the spirit of the devil, which worketh in the children of disobedience, Eph. 2:1-3.

But do they believe that it is so with them? No! They are in their own accounts, as other madmen are, the only ones in the world: hence they are so taken and pleased with their own frantic notions, that they deride all else that dwell in the world.

But what makes one that is wild, or a mad man, sober? To let him alone will not do it. To give him good words only will not do it. No! He must be tamed. Some means must be used to tame him. "He brought down their heart with labour," or by continual harassment as you have it, Ps. 107:10-12. He speaks there of mad men that are deep in darkness and "bound in afflictions and iron, because they rebelled against the words of God, and contemned the counsel of the Most High."

This, therefore, is the way to deal with such, and none but God can deal with them. They must be taken, and separated from men. They must be laid in chains, in darkness, afflictions, and irons. They must be bled, half-starved, whipped, purged, and be dealt with as mad people are dealt with. And thus they must be dealt with until they come to themselves, and cry out in their distresses. "And then they [cry] to the Lord in their troubles, and He [saveth] them out of their distresses": then He brings them "out of darkness and the shadow of death, and [breaks] their bands in sunder," Ps. 107:13,14.

Thus, I say, God tames the world, and brings mad prodigals to themselves, and so to Him for mercy.

Ninthly, Man, as he comes into the world, is not only a dead man, but also a fool, proud, self-willed, fearless and a false believer, he is a lover of sin, and a wild man, but a man that wrongly discerns and does not enjoy the things of the kingdom of God. I told you before that the unconverted man is such as did not taste things. But now I add that he judges things incorrectly. He calls bitter *sweet*, and sweet *bitter*; he judges quite amiss. These are they God threatened with a woe: "Woe unto them that call evil good, and good evil; that put darkness for light, and light for darkness; that put bitter for sweet, and sweet for bitter!" Isa. 5:20.

This latter part of this text shows us evidently that the things of God are evaluated inappropriately by some. They call his sweet things bitter, and the devil's bitter things sweet; and all this is for want of a broken heart. A broken heart discerns things differently than a whole or unbroken one does.

A man that has no pain or bodily distress cannot find or feel value or good in the cast applied to arm or leg. No, he rather says, Away with these stinking, smudgy things! Oh! but apply this plaster cast to where there is need, and the patient will appreciate and taste, and savour the goodness of them. He will prize and commend them to others.

Thus it is in spiritual things. The world does not know what the anguish or pain of a broken heart means. They say, "Who will show us any good?" we are better off to find it in our sports, pleasures, estates, and entertainments. "There be many," says the Psalmist, speak after this sort. But what says the distressed man? Why, "Lord, lift Thou up the light of Thy countenance upon us"; and then adds, "Thou hast put gladness in my heart," namely, by the "light of Thy countenance"; for that is the plaster for a broken heart. "Thou hast put gladness in my heart, more than in the time that their corn and their wine increased," Ps. 4:6,7.

Oh! a broken heart can enjoy pardon, can appreciate the comfort of the Holy Ghost, even as a hungry or thirsty man prizes bread and water in the lack thereof. So the broken in heart prize and sets a high esteem on the things of the Lord Jesus. His flesh, His blood, His promise, and the light of His countenance are the only sweet things both to scent and taste, to those that are of a wounded spirit. The full soul loathes the honey-comb. The whole despise the Gospel, they do not appreciate the things that are of God.

If twenty men were to hear a pardon read, and only one of those twenty was condemned to die, which of these men do you think would taste the sweetness of that pardon? Would it be they who were not guilty or he that was condemned? The condemned man, doubtless.

This is the case in hand. The broken in heart is a condemned man. Yes, it is a sense of condemnation, with other things, that has indeed broken his heart; nor is there anything but a sense of forgiveness that can bind it up or heal it. But could that heal it, could he not taste, truly taste, or rightly enjoy forgiveness? No: forgiveness would be to him as it is to him that has not a sense of need of it.

But, I say, what is the reason some so prize what others so despise, since they both stand in need of the same grace and mercy of God in Christ? Why, the one sees, and the other sees not this woeful, miserable state. And thus have I showed you the necessity of a broken heart.

1. Man is dead, and must be quickened.

2. Man is a fool, and must be made wise.

3. Man is proud, and must be humbled.

4. Man is self-willed, and must be broken.

5. Man is fearless, and must be made to consider.

6. Man is a false believer, and must be rectified.

7. Man is a lover of sin, and must be weaned from it.

8. Man is wild, and must be tamed.

9. Man misjudges the things of God, and can take no enjoyment in them until his heart is broken.

The Acceptable Sacrifice

And thus I have done with this, and shall next come to the reasons of the point; namely, to show you why or how it comes to pass that a broken heart, a heart truly contrite, is to God such an excellent thing.

Chapter 4

Why a Broken Heart Is Esteemed by God As an Excellent Thing

FIRST, *A broken heart is the handiwork of God. It is a heart of His own preparing, for His own service. It is a sacrifice of His own providing, of His providing for himself.* As Abraham said, in another case, "God will provide himself a lamb," Gen. 22:8.

Hence it is said, The preparation of the heart in man is from the Lord. And again, "God maketh my heart soft, and the Almighty troubleth me," Job 23:16.

The heart, as it is by nature hard, stupid, and impenetrable, so it remains and so will remain, until God, as was said, bruises it with His hammer and melts it with His fire.

The stony nature of it therefore is said to be taken away of God: "I will take away the stony heart out of your flesh, and will give you," saith He, "an heart of flesh," Ezek. 36:26.

"I will take away the stony heart," or the stoniness, or the hardness of your heart, "and I will give you an heart of flesh"; that is, I will make your heart sensible, soft, wieldable, governable, and penitent. Sometimes

He bids men rend their hearts, not because they can, but to convince them rather, that, though it must be so, they cannot do it. So He bids them make themselves a new heart and a new spirit for the same purpose also; for if God does not break it, it remains unbroken: if God makes it not new, it abides an old one still.

This is what is meant by His bending of men for himself, and of His working in them that which is pleasing in His sight, Zech. 9:13.

The heart, soul, or spirit, as in itself, as it came from God's fingers, is a precious thing, a thing, in God's account, worth more than all the world. Sin has hardened his heart, soul, or spirit. The devil has bewitched and the world has deceived it. This heart, thus beguiled, God longs for and desires: "My son," saith He, "give me thine heart, and let thine eyes observe My ways," Prov. 23:26.

This man cannot do this thing, since his heart, having the mastery of him, will not but lead him into all manner of vanity. What now must be done? God must take the heart by storm, by power, and bring it to a compliance with the Word. But the heart of itself will not. It is deluded, carried away to another than God. Wherefore, God now forces him to wave his sword, and brings down the heart with labour. He opens it, and drives out "the strong man armed" that did keep it. He wounds it, and makes it hurt for its rebellion, that it may cry. So He rectifies it for himself: "He maketh sore, and bindeth up; He woundeth, and His hands make whole," Job 5:18.

Thus, having made it for himself, it becomes His habitation, His dwelling place: "That Christ may dwell in your hearts by faith," Eph. 3:17.

But I would not swerve from the thing in hand. I have told you a broken heart is the handiwork of God, a sacrifice of His own preparing, a material fitted for himself.

1. By breaking the heart, He opens it, and makes it a receptacle for the graces of His Spirit; that is, the cabinet, when unlocked, where God lays up the jewels of the Gospel. There He puts His fear: "I will put My fear in their heart." There He writes His law: "I will write My law in their

58

heart." There he puts His Spirit: "I will put My Spirit within you," Jer. 32:39-40; 31:31-33; Ezek. 36:26,27.

This heart God chooses for His cabinet. There He hides His treasure, there is the seat of justice, mercy, and of every grace of God. I mean when it is broken, made contrite, and so regulated by the holy Word.

2. The heart, when broken, is like sweet gums and spices when beaten. For, as such they cast their fragrant scent into the nostrils of men. So the heart, when broken, casts its sweet smells into the nostrils of God. The incense, which was a type of prayer of old, was to be beaten or bruised, and so to be burned in the censer. The heart must be beaten or bruised, and then the sweet scent will come out, groaning, and crying, and sighing for the mercy of God. Its cries, to Him, are a very excellent thing, and pleasing in His nostrils.

Secondly, *A broken heart is in the sight of God an excellent thing, because a broken heart is submissive.* It falleth before God, and gives to Him His glory. All this is true from a multitude of scriptures which I need not here mention. Such an heart is called an honest heart, a good heart, a perfect heart, a heart fearing God, and such as is sound in God's statutes.

Now, this must be an excellent thing, if we consider that by such an heart unfeigned obedience is yielded unto Him that calls for it. "Ye have obeyed from the heart," says Paul to them at Rome, "that form of doctrine which was delivered you," Rom. 6:17.

Alas! the heart, before it is broken and made contrite, is of quite another nature. It is "not subject to the law of God, neither indeed can be," Rom. 8:7. The great battle before the heart is broken, is about who shall be lord, God or the sinner. True, the right of dominion is the Lord's; but the sinner will not allow it, but will be all himself, saying, "Who is lord over us?" And again, say they to God, "We are lords; we will come no more unto Thee," Ps. 12:4; Jer. 2:31.

This also is evident by their practice. God may say what He will, but they will do what they prefer. "Keep My Sabbath," says God. "I will not," says the sinner. "Leave your whoring," says God. "I will not," says the sinner. "Do not tell lies, nor swear, nor curse, nor blaspheme My holy name," says God. "Oh, but I will," says the sinner. "Turn to Me," says God. "I will not," says the sinner. "The right of dominion is Mine," says God. But, like that young rebel, 1 Kings 1:5, "I will be king," says the sinner. Now, this is intolerable, this is insufferable, and every sinner by practice says thus, for they have not submitted themselves unto the righteousness of God.

There can be no concord, no communion, no agreement, no fellowship: There is enmity on the one side, and flaming justice on the other, 2 Cor. 6:14-16; Zech. 11:8.

And what delight, what content, what pleasure can God take in such men? None at all. No, though they should be mingled with the best of the saints of God. Though the best of saints should supplicate for them. "Thus," says Jeremiah, "said the Lord unto me, Though Moses and Samuel stood before Me," that is, to pray for them, "yet My mind could not be toward this people: cast them out of My sight, and let them go forth," Jer. 15:1.

Here is nothing else but open war, acts of hostility, and shameful rebellion on the sinner's side; and what delight can God take in that? Wherefore, if God will bend and buckle the spirit of such an one, He must shoot an arrow at him, a bearded arrow, such as may not be plucked out of the wound—an arrow that will stick fast (Ps. 38:1,2), and cause that sinner to fall down as dead at God's foot; then will the sinner deliver up his arms, and surrender up himself as one conquered, into the hand of, and beg for the Lord's pardon, and not till then; I mean, not sincerely.

And now God has overcome, and His right hand and His holy arm has gotten Him the victory. Now He rides in triumph, with His captive at His chariot-wheel: now He glories. How the bells in heaven do ring. How the angels shout for joy, yea, are bid to do so: "Rejoice with me, for I have found my sheep which was lost," Luke 15:1-10.

Now, also, the sinner, as a token of being overcome, lies groveling at His foot saying, "Thine arrows are sharp in the heart of the King's enemies, whereby the people fall under Thee," Ps. 45:5.

Now the sinner submits. Now he follows his conqueror in chains. Now he seeks peace, and would give all the world, were it his own, to be in the favor of God, and to have hopes by Christ of being saved.

Now, this must be pleasing, this cannot but be a thing acceptable in God's sight. "A broken and contrite heart, O God, Thou wilt not despise." It is the desire of his own heart, the work of his own hands.

Thirdly, *Another reason why a broken heart is to God such an excellent thing is this: a broken heart prizes Christ, and has an high esteem for Him.* The whole have no need of the physician, but the sick. This sick man is the broken-hearted in the text. God makes men sick by the smiting of them, by breaking of their hearts. Hence sickness and wounds are put together, for that the one is a true effect of the other, Mk. 2:17; Mic. 6:13; Hos. 5:13.

Can any think that God should be pleased when men despise His Son, saying, "He hath no form nor comeliness; and when we shall see Him, there is no beauty that we should desire Him?" And yet so say they of him whose heart God has not softened. The elect themselves confess, that before their hearts were broken, they set light by Him also. He is, say they, "Despised and rejected of men...and we hid as it were our faces from Him; He was despised, and we esteemed Him not," Isa. 53:2,3.

He is indeed the great deliverer. But what is a deliverer to them that never saw themselves in bondage, as was said before? Hence it is said of him that delivered the city, "No man remembered that same poor man," Eccles. 9:14,15.

He has sorely suffered, and been bruised for the transgression of men, that they might not receive the hurt and hell which, by their sins, they have procured to themselves. But what is that to them that never saw anything but beauty, and that never tasted anything but sweetness in sin?

It is He that holds, by His intercession, the hands of God, and that causes Him to forbear and not to cut off the drunkard, the liar, and unclean person, even when they are in the very act and work of their abomination. But their hard heart, their stupefied heart, has no sense of such kindness as this, and therefore they take no notice of it. How many times has God said to this dresser of His vineyard, "Cut down the barren fig-tree"; while he yet, by his intercession, has prevailed for a reprieve for another year? But no notice is taken of this. No thanks are returned to Him for such kindness of Christ. Wherefore, such ungrateful, inconsiderate wretches as these must needs be a continual eye-sore, as I may say, and great provocation to God: and yet thus men will do before their hearts are broken, Luke 13:6-9.

Christ, as I said, is called a Physician. Yes, He is the only soul Physician: He heals, however desperate the disease be; yes, and heals all whom He undertakes, for ever: "I give unto them eternal life," John 10:28, and doth all of free cost, of mere mercy and compassion.

But what is all this to one that sees not his sickness and sees nothing of a wound? What is the best physician alive, or all the physicians in the world, put all together, to him that knows no sickness, that is sensible of no disease? Physicians, as was said, may go seeking the healthful. Physicians are of no honor save only to the sick, or upon a supposition of being so, now or at any other time.

This is the reason why Christ is so little accepted in the world. God has not made them sick by smiting of them. His sword has not given them the wound, His dart has not been struck through their liver, they have not been broken with His hammer, nor melted with His fire. So they have no regard to His Physician. So they disregard all the provision which God has made for the salvation of the soul.

But now, let such a soul be wounded. Let such a man's heart be broken. Let such a man be made sick through the sting of guilt, and be made to wallow in ashes under the burden of his transgressions, and then, who but Christ can heal them? As has been shown before, only the Physician. "Wash me, Lord; supple my wounds; then pour Thy wine and oil into my sore; then, Lord Jesus, cause me to hear the voice of joy and gladness, that the bones which Thou hast broken may rejoice." Nothing is now so welcome as healing, and so, nothing so desirable as Christ. His name to such is the best of names. His love to such is the best of love, himself being now, not only in himself, but also to such a soul, "the chiefest among ten thousand," Song 5:10.

As bread to the hungry, as water to the thirsty, as sight to the blind, and liberty to the imprisoned, so, and a thousand times more, is Jesus Christ to the wounded, and to them that are broken-hearted.

Now, as was said, this must be excellent in God's eyes, since Christ Jesus is so glorious in His eyes. To consider with contempt what a man counts excellent is an offence to him. But to value, esteem, or think highly of that which is of honor with me, this is pleasing to me. Such an opinion is excellent in my sight.

What does Christ say? "[My] Father himself loveth you, because ye have loved Me." Who has an high honor for Christ, the Father has a high honor for them. Hence it is said, He that hath the Son, hath the Father: the Father will be his, and will do for him as a father who receiveth and sets an honourable esteem on his son, John 16:27.

But none will, none can, do this but the broken-hearted, because they, and they only, are sensible of the lack and worth of an interest in Him.

I appeal to all the world as to the truth of this, and do say again, that these, and none but these, have hearts of esteem in the sight of God. Alas! "the heart of the wicked is little worth," Prov. 10:20, for it is destitute of a precious esteem of Christ, and cannot but be destitute, because it is not wounded, broken, and made sensible of the lack of mercy by Him.

Fourthly, *A broken heart is of great esteem with God, because it is a thankful heart for that sense of sin and of grace it has received.*

The broken heart is a sensitive heart. This we touched upon before. It is sensitive of the dangers which sin leads to, and has cause to be sensitive thereof, because it has seen and felt what sin is, both in the guilt and punishment that by law is due thereto. As a broken heart is sensitive of sin in the evil nature and consequences of it, so it is also sensitive of the way of God's delivering the soul from the day of judgment; consequently it must be a thankful heart. Now, "Whoso offereth praise glorifieth Me," saith God; and God loves to be glorified; God's glory is dear unto Him, He will not part with that. Ps. 50:23; Isa. 42:8.

The broken-hearted, say I, forasmuch as he is the sensitive soul, it follows that he is the thankful soul. "Bless the Lord, O my soul," said David, "and all that is within me, bless His holy name." Behold what blessing of God is here! and yet, not content herewith, he goes on with it again, saying, "Bless the Lord, O my soul, and forget not all His benefits," Ps. 103:1,2. But what is the matter? Oh, He has forgiven all thine iniquities, and healed all thy diseases. He has redeemed thy life from destruction, and crowneth thee with loving-kindness and tender mercies, ver. 3,4. But how did he come to be affected with this? Why, he knew what it was to hang over the mouth of hell for sin. He knew what it was for death and hell to beset and surround him. They took hold of him, as we have said, and were pulling him down into the deep. This he saw, to the breaking of his heart. He saw also the way of life, and had his soul relieved with faith and sense of that, and that made him a thankful man. If a man who has had a broken leg is made to understand, that by the breaking of that, he kept from breaking his neck, he will be thankful to God for a broken leg. "It is good for me," said David, "that I have been afflicted"; I was by that preserved from a great danger; for before that, I went astray, Ps. 119:67,71.

And who can be thankful for a mercy, that is not aware that they want it, have it, and have it of mercy. Now, this is the broken-hearted. This is the man that is of a contrite spirit. He is aware of the mercies of the best sort, and therefore must needs be a thankful man, and so have an heart of esteem with God, because it is a thankful heart.

Fifthly, *A broken heart is of great esteem with, or an excellent thing in the sight of, God, because it is an heart that desires now to become a receptacle or habitation for the spirit and graces of the spirit of God.*

It was the devil's hold before, and was contented so to be. But now it is for entertaining of and for being possessed with, the Holy Spirit of

64

God. "Create in me a clean heart," said David, "and renew a right spirit within me...take not Thy Holy Spirit from me...uphold me with thy free Spirit," Ps. 51:10-12.

Now he wants a clean heart and a right spirit. How he longs for the sanctifyings of the blessed Spirit of grace, a thing which the uncircumcised in heart resist and do despite unto, Acts 7:51; Heb. 10:29.

A broken heart, therefore, fits with the heart of God. A contrite spirit is one spirit with Him. God, as I told you before, covets to dwell with the broken in heart, and the broken in heart desireth communion with Him. Now here is an agreement, a oneness of mind. The same mind is in you which was also in Christ Jesus. This must needs be an excellent spirit. This must needs be better with God, and in His sight, than thousands of rams or ten thousand rivers of oil.

But does the carnal world covet this, this Spirit and the blessed graces of it? No; they despise it, as I said before. They mock at it; they prefer and reflect any sorry, dirty lust. The reason is, because they lack a broken heart, that heart so highly in esteem with God, and remain, for lack thereof, in their enmity to God.

The broken heart is to become a habitation for the Spirit of God.

The broken-hearted knows that the workings of the Spirit are a good means to keep from that relapse out of which a man cannot come unless his heart be wounded a second time. Doubtless, David had a broken heart at first conversion, and if that brokenness had remained, that is, had he not given way to hardness of heart again, he would have never fallen into that sin out of which he could not be recovered but by the breaking of his bones a second time. Therefore, I say, a broken heart is of great esteem with God for, I will add, so long as it retains its tenderness. It covets none but God and the things of the Holy Spirit. Sin is an abomination to it.

Advantages of a Tender Heart

And here, it befits me to say before I go any further, that I will show you some of the advantages that a Christian gets by keeping of his heart tender.

The Acceptable Sacrifice

As to have a broken heart is to have an excellent thing, so to keep this broken heart tender is also very advantageous.

First, This is the way to maintain in your soul always a fear of sinning against God. Christians do not wink at, or give way to sin, until their hearts begin to lose their tenderness. A tender heart will be afflicted at the sin of another. Much more it will be afraid of committing sin itself, 2 Kings 22:19.

Secondly, A tender heart quickly yields to prayer, even prompteth to it, puts an edge and fire into it. We never are backward to prayer until our heart has lost its tenderness, though then it grows cold, flat, and formal, and so carnal *to* and *in* that holy duty.

Thirdly, A tender heart is always quick to repent for the least fault, or slip, or sinful thought that the soul is guilty of. In many things the best of us offend. But if a Christian loses his tenderness, if he says he has no repentance, his heart is grown hard, and has lost that spirit, that kind spirit of repentance it was wont to have. Thus it was with the Corinthians; they were decayed, and lost their tenderness; wherefore their sin, yea, great sins, remained unrepented of, 2 Cor. 12:20,21.

Fourthly, A tender heart longs to renew often its communion with God, when he that is hardened, though the seed of grace is in him, will be content to eat, drink, sleep, wake, and go days without number without Him, Isa. 17:10,11; Jer. 2:32.

Fifthly, A tender heart is a wakeful, watchful heart. It watches against sin in the soul, sin in the family, sin in the calling, sin in spiritual duties and performances, etc. It watches against Satan, against the world, against the flesh, etc.

But now, when the heart is not tender, there is sleepiness, unwatchfulness, idleness, a suffering heart, the family, and calling to be much defiled, spotted, and blemished with sin; for a heart departs from God, and turns aside in all these things.

Sixthly, A tender heart will deny itself, even in lawful things, and will forbear even that which may be done, lest some Jew, or Gentile, or the

66

church of God, or any member of it, should be offended or made weak thereby. Whereas the Christian that is not tender, that has lost his tenderness, is so far beyond being able to deny himself in lawful things, that he will even adventure to meddle in things utterly forbidden, no matter who is offended, grieved, or made weak thereby. For example, we need go no further than to the man in the text, who, while he was tender, trembled at little things; but when his heart was hardened, he could take Bathsheba to satisfy his lust, and kill her husband to cover his wickedness.

Seventhly, A tender heart, I mean the heart kept tender, is preserved from many a blow, lash, and fatherly chastisement, because it shuns the causes (which is sin) of the scourging hand of God. "With the pure Thou wilt show Thyself pure; and with the froward Thou wilt show Thyself unsavoury," 2 Sam. 22:27; Ps. 18:25,26.

Many a needless rebuke and wound does happen to the saints of God through their unwise behaviour. When I say needless, I mean they are not necessary, but to bring us back from our vanities. For we should not feel the smart of them were it not for our follies. Hence the afflicted is called a fool, because his folly brings his affliction upon him. "Fools," says David, "because of their transgression, and because of their iniquities, are afflicted," Ps. 107:17; and therefore it is, as was said before, that he calls his sin his foolishness. And again, "[God] will speak peace unto His people, and to His saints; but let them not turn again to folly," Ps. 38:5; 85:8. If his children transgress My laws, I will visit their transgressions with a rod, and their iniquities with stripes.

But what should a Christian do, when God has broken his heart, to keep it tender?

To this I will speak briefly. And,
First, Give you several cautions.
Secondly, Several directions.
For cautions,

1. Take heed that you do not choose those convictions that at present do break your hearts, by laboring to put those things out of your minds which were the cause of such convictions. Rather nourish and

cherish those things in a deep and sober remembrance of them. Think, therefore, with thyself thus: What was it that first wounded my heart? And let that still be there until by the grace of God and the redeeming blood of Christ it is removed.

2. Shun vain company. The keeping of vain company has stifled many a conviction, killed many a desire, and made many a soul fall into hell that once was hot in looking after heaven. A companion that is not profitable to the soul is hurtful: "He that walketh with wise men shall be wise: but a companion of fools shall be destroyed," Prov. 13:20.

3. Take heed of idle talk, that you neither hear nor join with it. "Go from the presence of a foolish man, when thou perceivest not in him the lips of knowledge," Prov. 14:7. "Evil communications corrupt good manners;" and "a fool's...lips are the snare of his soul." Wherefore take heed of these things, 1 Cor. 15:33; Prov. 18:7.

4. Beware of the least movement to sin, that it be not looked upon, lest the looking upon it make way for a bigger sin. David's eye took his heart. So his heart, nourishing the thought, made way for the woman's company, the act of adultery, and bloody murder. "Take heed, brethren...lest any of you be hardened through the deceitfulness of sin." Heb. 3:12,13.

And remember that he who cuts a log must first put the thin end of the wedge thereto, and so, by driving, do his work.

5. Take heed of evil examples among the godly. Don't learn from man how to do that which the Word of God forbids. Sometimes Satan makes use of a good man's bad ways to spoil and harden the heart of them that come after. Peter's false doings spoiled Barnabas, and several others. Wherefore take heed of men, of *good* men's ways, and measure both theirs and thine own by no other rule but the holy Word of God, Gal. 2:11-13.

6. Take heed of unbelief, or atheistic thoughts. Make no question of the truth and reality of heavenly things. Know this that unbelief is the worst of evils; nor can the heart be tender that nourishes or gives place

unto it. "Take heed, brethren, lest there be in any of you an evil heart of unbelief, in departing from the living God," Heb. 3:12.

These cautions are necessary to be observed with all diligence of all them that would, when their heart is made tender, keep it so.

And now to come to the directions.

1. Seek after a deep knowledge of God, to keep it warm upon thy heart. Knowledge of His presence, that is, everywhere: "Do not I fill heaven and earth? saith the Lord," Jer. 23:24.

2. Knowledge of His piercing eye, that it runs to and fro through the earth, beholding in every place the evil and the good; that His eyes behold, and His eyelids try the children of men, Prov. 15:3; Ps. 11:4.

3. The knowledge of His power, that He is able to turn and dissolve heaven and earth into dust and ashes, and that they are in His hand but as a scroll or vesture, Heb. 1:11,12.

4. The knowledge of His justice, that the rebukes of it are as devouring fire, Heb. 12:29.

5. The knowledge of His faithfulness, in fulfilling promises to them to whom they are made, and of His threatenings on the impenitent, Mt. 5:18; 24:35; Mk. 13:31.

Secondly, work hard to get and keep a deep sense of sin in its evil nature, and in its soul-destroying effects upon our heart. Be persuaded that it is the only enemy of God, and that none hate, or are hated of God, but through that.

1. Remember, it turned angels into devils; thrust them down from heaven into hell.

2. It is the chain in which they are held and bound over to judgment, 2 Pet. 2:4; Jude 6.

3. It was for that that Adam was turned out of Paradise; that for which the old world was drowned; that for which Sodom and Gomorrah

were burned with fire from heaven; and that which cost Christ His blood to redeem thee from the curse it has brought upon thee; and that, if any thing, will keep thee out of heaven for ever and ever.

4. Consider the pains of hell. Christ makes use of that as an argument to keep the heart tender, even to that end, repeats and repeats both the nature and durableness of the burning flame thereof, and of the gnawing of the never-dying worm that dwells there, Mark 9:43-48.

Thirdly, Consider of death, both as to the certainty of thy dying, and uncertainty of the time when. We must die, we must needs die, our days are determined, the number of our months are with God, though not with us; nor can we pass them, even though we would give a thousand worlds to do it, 2 Sam. 14:14; Job 7:1; 14:1-5.

Consider that you must die but once. I mean but once as to this world. For if you, when you go hence, do not die well, then you cannot come back again and die better. "It is appointed unto men once to die, but after this the judgment," Heb. 9:27.

Fourthly, Consider also the certainty of terribleness of the day of judgment, when Christ shall sit upon His great white throne; when the dead shall, by the sound of the trump of God, be raised up; when the elements, with heaven and earth, shall be on a burning flame; when Christ shall separate men one from another, as a shepherd divides his sheep from the goats; when the books shall be opened, the witness produced, and every man be judged according to his works; when heaven-gate shall stand open to them that shall be saved, and the jaws of hell stand gaping for them that shall be damned. Acts 17:30,31; 10:42; Mt. 25:30,31; Rev. 2:11; 1 Cor. 15:51,52; Rev. 20:12; 2 Pet. 3:7,10,12; Mt. 25:32; Rom. 2:2,15,16; Rev. 22:12; Mt. 25:34,41; Rev. 20:15.

Fifthly, Consider, Christ Jesus did use no means to harden His heart against doing and suffering those sorrows which were necessary for the redemption of your soul. Rather, He (though He could have hardened His heart against thee in the way of justice and righteousness, because you had sinned against Him), He awakened himself, and put on all pity, bowels, and compassion, even, tender mercies, and did it. In His love and in

70

His pity He saved us. His tender mercy from on high has visited us; He loves us, and gave himself for us.

Learn from Christ to be tender of yourself, and to endeavor to keep your heart tender towards God and to the salvation of your soul.

Conclusion

LET us now, then, make some practical use of this doctrine.

First, From the truth of the matter; namely, that the man who is *truly* come to God has had his heart broken, that is, his heart broken in order to his coming to Him. This shows us what to judge of the word that is between sin and the soul: to wit, that it is so firm, so strong, so inviolable, as that nothing can break, disannul, or make it void, unless the heart be broken for it. It was so with David; even his new word with it could not be broken until his heart was broken.

It is amazing to consider what hold sin has on some men's souls, spirits, will, and affections. It is to them better than heaven, better than God, than the soul, even than salvation. It is evident, because, though all these are offered them upon this condition, if they will but leave their sins, yet they will choose rather to abide by them, to stand and fall by them. How sayest thou, sinner? is not this truth? How many times have you had heaven and salvation offered to you freely, if you would but break thy connection with this great enemy of God? Of God, do I say? if you would but break this link with this great enemy of your soul; but you never could yet be brought unto it: no, neither by threatening nor by promise could you ever yet be brought unto it.

The Acceptable Sacrifice

It is said of Ahab, "[He sold] himself to work wickedness;" and in another place, "Behold, for your iniquities have ye sold yourselves," 1 Kings 21:25; Isa. 50:1.

But what is this iniquity? Why, a thing of nothingness, nay, worse than nothingness a thousand times, but because nothing is, as we say, nothing; therefore it goes under that term where God saith again to the people, "Ye have sold yourselves for nought," Isa. 52:3.

But, I say, what an amazing thing is this, that a rational creature should make no better a bargain; that one that is so wise in all earthly things should be such a fool in the thing that is most weighty; and yet such a fool he is, and he tells every one that goes by the way that he is such an one, because he will not break his bond with sin until his heart is broken for it.

Men love darkness rather than light. They make it manifest that they love it, since so great an offer will not prevail with them to leave it.

Secondly, Is this a truth, that the man that truly comes to God in order thereto, has had his heart broken? Then this shows us a reason why some men's hearts are broken, even a reason why God breaks some men's hearts for sin, namely, because He would not have them die in it, but rather come to God that they might be saved.

Behold therefore, how God resolved to save some men's souls. He will have them, He will save them, He will break their hearts, but He will save them. He will kill them that they may life.

He will wound them that He may heal them.

He will wound us that He may heal us.

And it seems, by our discourse, that now there is no way left but this. Fair means, as we say, will not do. Good words, a glorious Gospel, entreatings, beseeching with blood and tears, will not do. Men are resolved to put God to the utmost of it. If He will have them, He must fetch them, follow them, catch them, lame them, even break their bones, or else He shall not save them.

74

Conclusion

Some men think an invitation is an outward call, that a rational discourse will do; but they are much deceived. There must be a power, an exceeding great and mighty power, attend the Word, or it works not effectually to the salvation of the soul. I know these things are enough to leave men without excuse. But they are not enough to bring men home to God. Sin has hold of them, and they have sold themselves to it. The power of the devil has hold of them, and they are his captives at his will. More than all this, their will is one with sin and with the devil, to be held captive thereby; and if God does not give contrition, repentance, or a broken heart for sin, then man will not have so much as a mind in him to forsake this so horrible a confederacy and plot against his soul, 2 Tim. 2:25,26.

Hence men are said to be drawn from these breasts, that come, or that are brought to Him, Isa. 28:9; John 6:44.

Wherefore John might well say, "Behold, what manner of love the Father hath bestowed upon us!" 1 Jn. 3:1. Here is cost bestowed, pains bestowed, labor bestowed, repentance bestowed, even a heart made sore, wounded, broken, and filled with pain and sorrow, in order to bring forth the salvation of the soul.

Thirdly, This, then, may teach us what estimation to set upon a broken heart. A broken heart is such as God honors, even as God counts better than all external service. A broken heart is that which is necessary for salvation, and to your coming to Christ for life.

The world does not know what to make of it nor what to say to one that has a broken heart. Therefore they despise it, and count that man that carries it in his bosom a moping fool, a miserable wretch, an undone soul. But "a broken and a contrite spirit, O God, Thou wilt not despise." A broken heart takes Your eye, Your heart. You choose it for Your companion, and have given Your Son a charge to look well to such a man, and hast promised him His salvation, as has before been proved.

Sinner, have you obtained a broken heart? Has God bestowed a contrite spirit upon you? He has given you what He himself is pleased with. He has given you a cabinet to hold his grace in. He has given you an heart that can heartily desire His salvation, an heart after His own heart; that is, such as suits His mind.

True, it is painful now, sorrowful now, penitent now, grieved now; now it is broken, now it bleeds, now it sobs, now it sighs, now it mourns and cries unto God. Well, very well, all this is because He has a mind to make you laugh. He has made you sorry on earth, that you might rejoice in heaven. "Blessed are [ye] that mourn, for [ye] shall be comforted: blessed are ye that weep now, for ye shall laugh," Mt. 5:4; Luke 6:21.

But, soul, be sure you have this broken heart. All hearts are not broken hearts, nor is every heart that seems to have a wound an heart that is *truly* broken. A man may be cut, yet not *into* the heart. A man may have another, yet not a broken heart, Acts 7:54; 1 Sam. 10:9. We know there is a difference between a wound in the flesh and a wound in the spirit—(*A man's sin may be wounded, and yet his heart not be broken.*) So was Pharaoh's, so was Saul's, so was Ahab's; but they had none of them the mercy of a broken heart. Therefore, I say, take heed—every scratch with a needle, every prick with a thorn, and every blow that God gives with His Word upon the heart of sinners does not therefore break them. God gave Ahab such a blow that He made him stoop, fast, humble himself, gird himself with, and lie in sackcloth, (which was a great matter for a king), and go softly; and yet he never had a broken heart, 1 Kings 21:27,29.

What shall I say? Pharaoh and Saul confessed their sin, Judas repented himself of his doings. Esau sought the blessing, and that carefully with tears; and yet none of these had an heart rightly broken, or a spirit truly contrite. Pharaoh, Saul, and Judas, were Pharaoh, Saul, and Judas still. Esau was Esau still. There was no gracious change, no thorough turn to God, no unfeigned parting with their sins, and no hearty flight for refuge, to lay hold on the hope of glory, though they indeed had thus been touched. Ex. 10:16; 1 Sam. 26:21; Mt. 27:3; Heb. 12:14-17.

The consideration of these things calls aloud to us to beware that we do not consider a broken and a contrite spirit that will not go for one at the day of death and judgment.

Conclusion

Wherefore, seeking soul, let me advise you, that you may not be deceived as to this thing of so great weight.

1. Go back towards the beginning of this book, and compare yourself with those six or seven signs of a broken and a contrite heart, which there I have according to the Word of God, given to you for that end; and deal with your soul impartially about them.

2. Consider what will be great help to you, if you will be sincere therein, namely, to make yourself search the Word, especially where you read of the conversion of men, and determine if your conversion be like, or has a good resemblance or oneness with theirs. In this be careful that, you do not compare yourself with those good folk of whose conversion you read not, or of the breaking of whose heart there is no mention made in Scripture. For all that are recorded in the Scripture as saints, do not have their conversion, as to the manner or nature of it, recorded in the Scripture.

3. Consider the true signs of repentance, which are laid down in Scripture, for that is the true effect of a broken heart and of a wounded spirit: and for this see Mt. 3:5,6; Luke 18:13; 19:8; Acts 2:37-40, etc.; 16:29,30; 19:18,19; 2 Cor. 7:8-11.

4. Take into consideration how God has said they shall be in their spirits, that He intends to save; and for this, read these Scriptures:

1. Read Jer. 31:9, "They shall come with weeping, and with supplications will I lead them," etc.

2. Read Jer. 50:4,5. "In those days, and in that time...the children of Israel shall come, they and the children of Judah together, going and weeping: they shall go and seek the Lord their God. They shall ask their way to Zion with their faces thitherward, saying, Come, and let us join ourselves to the Lord in a perpetual covenant that shall not be forgotten."

3. Read Ezek. 6:9. "And they that escape of you shall remember me among the nations, whither they shall be carried captives, because I am broken with their whorish heart, which hath departed from Me, and with their eyes, which go a whoring after their idols: and they shall loathe themselves for the evils which they have committed in all their abominations."

4. Read Ezek. 7:16. "But they that escape of them shall escape, and shall be on the mountains like doves of the valleys, all of them mourning, every one for his iniquity."

5. Read Ezek. 20:43. "And there shall ye remember your ways, and all your doings, wherein ye have been defiled; and ye shall loathe yourselves in your own sight for all your evils that ye have committed."

6. Read Ezek. 36:31. "Then shall ye remember your own evil ways, and your doings that were not good, and shall loathe yourselves in your own sight for your iniquities and for your abominations."

7. Read Zech. 12:10. "And I will pour upon the house of David, and upon the inhabitants of Jerusalem, the spirit of grace and of supplications; and they shall look upon Me whom they have pierced, and they shall mourn for Him, as one mourneth for his only son, and shall be in bitterness for Him, as one that is in bitterness for his firstborn."

Now, all these are the fruits of the Spirit of God, and of the heart when it is broken. Wherefore, soul, take notice of them: and, because these are texts by which God promises that those whom He saves shall have this heart, this Spirit, and these holy effects in them. Therefore consider again, and examine yourself whether this is the state and condition of your soul.

And that you may do it fully, consider again, and do thou,

1. Remember that here is such a sense of sin, and of the irksomeness thereof, as makes the man not only to abhor that, but himself because of that. This is worth noting.

2. Remember, again, that here is not only a self-abhorrence, but a sorrowful, kind mourning unto God at the consideration that the soul by sin has affronted, contemned, disregarded, and set at nought, both God and His holy Word.

3. Remember, also, that here are prayers and tears for mercy, with desires to be now out of love with sin for ever, and to be firmly joined and knit unto God in heart and soul.

4. Remember, also, that this people, here spoken of, have gone all the way, from Satan to God, from sin to grace, from death to life, scattered with tears and prayers, with weeping and supplication: "They shall go weeping and seeking the Lord their God."

5. Remember that these people, as strangers and pilgrims do, are not ashamed to ask the way, of those they meet with, to Zion or the heavenly country. They confess their ignorance, and their desire to know the way to life. Thereby they declare that there is nothing in this world, under the sun, or this side heaven, that can satisfy the longings, the desires, and cravings of a broken and contrite spirit.

Reader, be advised, and consider these things seriously, and compare your soul with them, and with what else you will find here written for your conviction and instruction.

Fourthly, If a broken heart and a contrite spirit be of such esteem with God, then this should encourage them that have it to come to God with it. I know the great encouragement for men to come to God is, that there is a "Mediator between God and men, the Man Christ Jesus," 1 Tim. 2:5. This, I say, is the great encouragement, and in its place there is none. There are other encouragements subordinate to that, and a broken and a contrite spirit is one of them. This is evident from several places of Scripture.

Wherefore, you that can carry a broken heart and a sorrowful spirit with you when you go to God, tell Him your heart is wounded within you, that you have sorrow in your heart, and are sorry for your sins. But take heed of lying. Confess also your sins unto Him, and tell Him they are continually before you. David made an argument of these things when he went to God by prayer. "O Lord," saith he, "rebuke me not in Thine anger, neither chasten me in Thy hot displeasure." But why so? Oh, says he, "Thine arrows stick fast in me, and Thy hand presseth me sore. There is no soundness in my flesh because of Thine anger; neither is there any rest in my bones because of my sin. For mine iniquities are gone over mine head: as an heavy burden they are too heavy for me. My wounds stink and are corrupt because of my foolishness. I am troubled; I am bowed down greatly; I go mourning all the day long. For my loins are filled with a loathsome disease: and there is no soundness in my flesh. I am feeble and sore broken: I have roared by reason of the disquietness of my heart. Lord, all my desire is before Thee; and my groaning is not hid from Thee. My heart panteth, my strength faileth me: as for the light of mine eyes, it also is gone from me. My lovers and my friends stand aloof from my sore." And so he goes on, Ps. 38:1-11, etc.

These are the words, sighs, complaints, prayers, and arguments of a broken heart to God for mercy; and so are these—"Have mercy upon me, O God, according to Thy lovingkindness: according unto the multitude of Thy tender mercies blot out my transgressions. Wash me thoroughly from mine iniquity, and cleanse me from my sin. For I acknowledge my transgressions: and my sin is ever before me," Ps. 51:1-3.

God allows poor creatures, that can without lying, thus to plead and argue with Him. "I am poor and sorrowful," said the good man to Him; "let Thy salvation, O God, set me up on high," Ps. 69:29.

Wherefore, you that have a broken heart, take courage; God bids you take courage: say, therefore, to your soul, "Why art thou cast down, O my soul," (as usually the broken-hearted are), "and why art thou disquieted within me? Hope thou in God. I had fainted unless I had believed to see the goodness of the Lord in the land of the living...Be of good courage, and He shall strengthen thine heart," Ps. 42:11; 43:5; 27:13,14.

But, alas! the broken-hearted are far off from this. They faint, they reckon themselves among the dead. They think God will remember them no more. The thoughts of the greatness of God, and His holiness, and their own sins and vilenesses, will certainly consume them. They feel guilt and anguish of soul. They go mourning all the day long. Their mouth is full of gravel and gall, and they are made to drink draughts of wormwood and gall. So that he must be an artist indeed at believing who can come to God under his guilt and horror, and plead in faith that the sacrifices of God are a broken heart, such as he has, and that a broken and a contrite spirit God will not despise.

Conclusion

Fifthly, If a broken heart, if a broken and a contrite spirit is of such esteem with God, then why should some be, as they are, so afraid of a broken heart, and so shy of a contrite spirit?

I have observed, that some men are as afraid of a broken heart, or that they for their sins should have their hearts broken, as the dog is of the whip. Oh, they cannot put up with such books, with such sermons, with such preachers, or with such talk as tends to make a man aware of, and to break his heart, and to make him contrite for his sins. Therefore they heap to themselves such teachers, get such books, love such company, and delight in such discourse that tends to harden rather than soften, to make desperate *in* rather than sorrowful *for* their sins. They say to such sermons, books, and preachers, as Amaziah said to Amos, "O thou seer, go, flee thee away into the land of Judah, and there eat bread, and prophesy there: but prophesy not again any more at Bethel," etc. Amos 7:12,13.

But do these people know what they do? Yes, think they. Such preachers, such books, such discourses, tend to make one melancholy or mad. They make us so that we cannot take pleasure in ourselves, in our concerns, in our lives.

But, O fool in grain! let me speak unto you. Is it a time to take pleasure, and to recreate thyself in any thing, before you have mourned and been sorry for your sins? That joy that is before repentance for sin will certainly end in heaviness. Wherefore the wise man, putting both together, says that mourning must be first: "There is a time to weep, and a time to laugh; a time to mourn, and a time to dance," Eccles. 3:4.

What! an unconverted man, and laugh? If you would hear one singing merry songs, that is riding up from Holborn to Tyburn to be hung for felony, wouldst thou not count him beside himself, if not worse? And yet thus it is with him that is for joy while he standeth condemned by the Book of God for his trespasses. Man, man, you have cause to mourn, even you *must* mourn, if ever you will be saved. Wherefore my advice is, that, instead of shunning, thou covet such books, such preachers, and such discourses as have a tendency to make a man aware of, and to break his heart for sin. The reason is, because you will never be as you should, concerned about, nor seek the salvation of your own soul, before you have a broken heart, a broken and a contrite spirit.

Wherefore, be not afraid of a broken heart. Be not shy of a contrite spirit. It is one of the greatest mercies that God bestows upon a man or a woman. The heart rightly broken at the sense of, and made truly contrite for, transgression is a certain forerunner of salvation. This is evident from these six demonstrations which were laid down to prove the point in hand at first.

And for thy awaking in this matter, let me tell thee, and thou wilt find it so, thou must have thy heart broken, whether thou wilt or no. God is resolved to break all hearts for sin some time or other.

Can it be imagined (sin being what it is, and God what He is, that is, a revenger of disobedience) but that one time or other man must hurt for sin: hurt, I say, either to repentance or to condemnation. He that mourns not now while the door of mercy is open, must mourn for sin when the door of mercy is shut.

Shall men despise God, break His law, place contempt on His threats, abuse His grace, even shut their eyes when He says, "See," and stop their ears when He says, "Hear," and shall they so escape? No, no: Because He called, and they refused—He stretched out His hand, and they regarded it not; therefore shall the calamity come upon them as one in travail, and they shall cry in their destruction; and then God "will laugh at [their] destruction, and mock when [their] fear cometh." Then, saith He, "They shall call," etc. Prov. 1:24-26, etc.

I have often observed that this threatening is repeated at least seven times in the New Testament, saying, "There shall be weeping and gnashing of teeth"; "there shall be wailing and gnashing of teeth"; as Mt. 8:12; 13:42,50; 22:13; 24:51; 25:30.

There! Where? In hell, and at the bar of Christ's tribunal, when He comes to judge the world, and shall have shut the door to keep them out of glory that have here despised the offer of His grace, and overlooked the day of His patience. "There shall be wailing and gnashing of teeth"; they shall weep and wail for this.

There are but two Scriptures that I shall use and then I shall draw towards a conclusion. One is that in Proverbs, where Solomon is counseling young men to beware of strange, that is, of wanton, light, and ensnaring women. Take heed of such, said he, lest "thou mourn at the last," that is, in hell, when you are dead, when your flesh and your body are consumed, and say, "How have I hated instruction, and my heart despised reproof; and have not obeyed the voice of my teachers, nor inclined mine ear to them that instructed me!" Prov. 5:1-13, etc.

The other Scripture is that in Isaiah, where he says, "Because when I called, ye did not answer; when I spake, ye did not hear; but did evil before Mine eyes, and did choose that wherein I delighted not. Therefore thus saith the Lord God, Behold, My servants shall eat, but ye shall be hungry: behold, My servants shall drink, but ye shall be thirsty: behold, My servants shall rejoice, but ye shall be ashamed: behold, My servants shall sing for joy of heart, but ye shall cry for sorrow of heart, and shall howl for vexation of spirit," Isa. 65:12-14.

How many beholds are here! And every behold is not only a call to careless ones to consider, but as a declaration from heaven, that thus at last it shall be with all impenitent sinners! that is, when others sing for joy in the kingdom of heaven, they shall sorrow in hell, and howl for vexation of spirit there.

Wherefore, let me advise that you be not afraid of, but that ye rather covet a broken heart, and prize a contrite spirit. I say, covet it now. Now the white flag is hung out. Now the golden secptre of grace is held forth to you. Better mourn now while God inclines to mercy and pardon, than mourn when the door is quite shut up. Take notice that this is not the first time that I have given you this advice.

Lastly, If a broken heart be a thing of so great esteem with God as has been said, and if duties cannot be rightly performed by a heart that has not been broken, then this shows the vanity of those people's minds, and also the invalidity of their pretended divine services, who worship

The Acceptable Sacrifice

God with an heart that was never broken, and without a contrite spirit. There have indeed at all times been great flocks of such professors in the world in every age, but to little purpose, unless to deceive themselves, to mock God, and lay stumbling-blocks in the way of others. For a man whose heart was never truly broken, and whose spirit was never contrite, cannot profess Christ in earnest, cannot love his own soul in earnest. I mean, he cannot do these things in truth, and seek his own good the right way, for he lacks a bottom for it. That is, a broken heart for sin, and a contrite spirit.

That which makes a man a hearty, an unfeigned, a sincere seeker after the good of his own soul, is a sense of sin and a godly fear of being overtaken with the danger which it brings a man into. This makes him contrite, or repentant, and makes him seek Christ the Saviour with heart-aching and heart-breaking considerations.

But this cannot be where this sense, this godly fear, and this holy contrition is lacking. Men may make noises, as the empty barrel makes the biggest sound. But prove them, and they are full of air, full of emptiness, and that is all.

Nor are such professors representative of God's name, nor of the credit of that gospel which they profess, nor can they be. For they lack that which should be for them thereunto, which is a sense of pardon and forgiveness; by the which their broken hearts would have been replenished, succoured, and made to hope in God. Paul said the love of Christ constrained him; but what was Paul but a broken-hearted and a contrite sinner? See Acts 9:3-6; 2 Cor. 5:14.

When God shows a man the sin he has committed, the hell he has deserved, the heaven he has lost, and shows him that Christ, and grace, and pardon may be had, this will make him serious. This will make him melt. This will break his heart. This will show him that there is more than air, than a noise, than an empty sound in religion. This is the man whose heart, whose life, whose conversation and all, will be engaged in the matters of the external salvation of his precious and immortal soul.

Conclusion

But some may object, that, in this saying, I seem too rigid and censorious, and will, if I do not moderate these lines with something milder afterwards, discourage many an honest soul.

I answer: Not a jot; not an honest soul in all the world will be offended at my words. For not one can be an honest soul, I mean with reference to its concerns in another world, that has not had a broken heart, that never had a contrite spirit. This I will say, because I would be understood aright, that all do not attain to the same degree of trouble, nor lie so long under, as some of their brethren do. But to go to heaven without a broken heart, or to be forgiven sin without a contrite spirit, is no article of my belief. We speak not now of what is secret. Revealed things belong to us and our children; nor must we venture to go further in our faith. Does not Christ say, "The whole have no need of the physician": they see no need. But Christ will make them see their need before He ministers His sovereign grace unto them. Good reason, otherwise He will have but little thanks for His kindness.

Answers to Objections

Objection. But there are some that have been godly educated from their childhood, and drink in the principles of Christianity in a way that they know not how.

Answer. I count it one thing to receive the faith of Christ from men only, and another to receive it from God by the means. If you are taught by an angel, yet, if not taught of God, you will never come to Christ. I do not say you will never profess Him. But if God speaks, and you will hear and understand Him, that voice will make such work within you as was never made before. The voice of God is a voice by itself, and is so distinguished by them that are taught thereby. Jn. 6:44,45; Ps. 29; Hab. 3:15,16; Eph. 4:20,21; 1 Pet. 2:2,3.

Objection. But some men are not so corrupted and profane as others, and therefore need not to be so hammered and fired as others; so broken and wounded as others.

Answer. God knows best what we need. Paul was as righteous before conversion as any that can pretend to civility now, I suppose; and

85

yet, that notwithstanding, he was made to shake, and was astonished at himself and at his conversion. And truly, I think, the more righteous any is in his own eyes before conversion, the more need he has of heart-breaking work, in order to his salvation, because a man is not by nature so easily convinced that his righteousness is to God abominable, as he is that is corrupted debauchery and profane.

A man's goodness is that which blinds him most; it is dearest to him, and hardly parted with; and therefore, when such an one is converted, that thinks he has goodness of his own enough to commend him in whole or in part to God (but few such are converted), there is required a great deal of breaking work upon his heart to make him come to Paul's conclusion, "What then? are we better than they? No, in no wise," (Rom. 3:9), I say, before he can be brought to see his glorious robes are filthy rages, and his gainful things but loss and dung. Isa. 64:6; Phil. 3.

This is also gathered from these words, "Publicans and the harlots go into the kingdom of God before [the Pharisees]," Mt. 21:31.

Why before them? but because they are closer to the word, are easier convinced of their need of Christ, and so are brought home to Him without, as I may say, all that ado that the Holy Ghost does make to bring home one of these to Him.

True, nothing is hard or difficult to God. But I speak after the manner of men. And let one who will, take to task a man corrupted in this life, and then one that is not so. He shall see, if he labors to convince them both that they are in a state of condemnation by nature, that the Pharisee will make his appeals to God with a great many "God I thank Thees," while the publican hangs down his head, shakes at heart, and smites upon his breast, "God be merciful to me a sinner," Lk. 18:11-13.

A self-righteous man is a devil in fine clothes.

Wherefore, a self-righteous man is but a painted Satan, or a devil in fine clothes.

But thinks he so of himself? No, no: he saith to others, Stand back, come not near me, "I am holier than thou." It is almost impossible that a self-righteous man should be saved; but he that can drive a camel through the eye of a needle, can cause that even such a one should see his lost condition, and that he needs the righteousness of God, which is by faith of Jesus Christ. He can make him see, I say, that his own goodness did stand more in his way to the kingdom of heaven than he was aware of. He can make him feel, too, that his leaning to that is as great iniquity as any immorality that men commit. The sum, then, is that men who are converted to God by Christ through the Word and Spirit (for all this must go to effectual conversion), must have their hearts broken, and their spirits made contrite. I say, it must be so, for the reason showed before.

All decayed, apostatized, and backslidden Christians must, in order to gain their recovery again to God, have their hearts broken, their souls wounded, their spirits made contrite, and become sorry for their sins.

Conversion to God is not so easy and so smooth a thing as some would have men believe it is. Why is man's heart compared to fallow ground, God's word to a plough, and his ministers to ploughmen, if the heart indeed has no need of breaking in order to the receiving of the seed of God unto eternal life? Jer. 4:3; Lk. 9:62; 1 Cor. 9:10.

Who knows not that fallow ground must be ploughed, and ploughed, too, before the husbandman will venture his seed; yes, and after that often soundly harrowed, or else he will have but a slender harvest?

Why is the conversion of the soul compared to the grafting of a tree, if that be done without cutting?

The Word is the graft, the soul is the tree, and the Word as the scion[1] must be let in by a wound; for to stick on the outside, or to be tied on with a string, will do no good here. Heart must be set to heart, and back to back, or your pretended engrafting will come to nothing, Rom. 11:17,24; Jas. 1:21.

I say, heart must be set to heart, and back to back, or the sap will not be transferred from the root to the branch; and I say, this must be done by a wound. The Lord opened the heart of Lydia, as a man opens

---

1.   Scion—the shoot of a plant joined to a stock in grafting.

87

the stock to graft in the scions, and so the Word was sent into her soul, and so the Word and her heart cemented and became one, Acts 16:14.

Why is Christ bid to gird His sword upon His thigh, and why must He make His arrows sharp, but that the heart may with this sword and these arrows be shot, wounded, and made to bleed? Why is He commanded to let it be so, if the people would bow and fall kindly under Him, and heartily implore His grace without it? Ps. 45:3-5.

Alas! men are too lofty, too proud, too wild, too devilishly resolved in the ways of their own destruction. In their life they are like the wild asses upon the wild mountains, nothing can break them of their purposes, or hinder them from ruining their own precious and immortal souls, but the breaking of their hearts.

Why is a broken heart put in the room of all sacrifices which we can offer to God, and a contrite spirit put into the room of all offerings, as they are (and you may see it so if you compare the text with that verse which goes before it); I say, why is it counted better than all, if they were all put together, if any one part, or if all external parts of worship, were they put together, could be able to render the man a sound and a rightly made new creature without it? "A broken heart, a contrite spirit, God will not despise"; but both you and all your service He will certainly slight and reject, if you come to Him without a broken heart. Wherefore, here is the point, come broken, come contrite, come aware *of* and sorry *for* your sins, or your coming will be counted no coming to God in the right way; and consequently you will get no benefit from it.

About the Author

One of the greatest of all the English Baptist preachers was John Bunyan. He was a great preacher of the gospel, a stalwart defender of the faith, and one of history's greatest authors. His life and writings are worth studying because they will prove to be an inspirational challenge to all.

John Bunyan was born near Bedford, which would become the birthplace of his future ministry, in the little town of Elstow in the year 1628. He was raised in the area and spent his entire life there. He was the son of a poor itinerant mender of pots and pans. Being the son of a tinker, as they were called, was a source of trouble as he was growing up because the Gypsies of England had been tinkers for many centuries, and many people felt that Bunyan must be of this alien blood. However, it has since been determined that Bunyan was actually of Norman ancestry.

Bunyan received little in the way of formal education. He left school at a very early age with only the barest knowledge of reading and writing, which he forgot soon after leaving. His love for fun was the main reason that he left school. This fun-loving attitude would get him in much trouble as the years went on.

Early in his life, Bunyan had a reverent fear of God. But as he grew older, his vivacious spirit often pulled him into sin. He was thrilled by rough sports and ball playing, which led him to break the Sabbath. His love for violence, and his coarse way of life eventually led to his becoming the leader of a local gang. As the leader of the gang, he gave time to "such reckless practices as the leadership of a crowd of reckless youths involves."[1] He was particularly noted for his swearing, blaspheming and lying. Although he was a reckless youth, at no time was he discovered drunk or promiscuous.

At the age of 16, Bunyan joined the Army. He spent two years in military service before returning home. Upon his return, his life was still aimless and full of turmoil. Finally, at the age of 19, he met an individual who would change his entire life—his future wife.

His bride was a poor, but godly woman who, as a dowry, had only two books. These two books were *Plain Man's Pathway to Heaven*, and *Practice of Piety*, both considered great favorites of the religious people of that time.[2] Bunyan, in order to please his wife, allowed her to read to him every night in order to teach him how to read. Finally, the message of these books began to sink in deep into his heart, although the outward change was not immediately recognizable.

On Sundays he dressed up and went to church both Sunday morning and Sunday evening. However, he was still a profane man. One Sunday, the pastor preached against Sabbath breaking, which left an impression on Bunyan and gave him much to consider. That very afternoon, as he was playing ball, he heard the voice of Jesus say to him, "Will you leave your sins and go to Heaven, or have your sins and go to hell?"[3]

This episode began a long, drawn out period of time when Bunyan battled against trusting in Christ as Savior. Finally, one afternoon in 1653, as he was walking through the woods, Bunyan suddenly realized the power of the grace of God and the hopelessness of his own condition.

---

1.   Thomas Armitage, *A History of the Baptists.* (New York: Bryan, Taylor and Co., 1887) 474.
2.   Austin Kennedy de Blois, *Fighters For Freedom.* (Philadelphia: Judson Press, 1929) 120.
3.   *Fighters*, 12.

Kneeling there, he accepted Christ as his personal Savior. His life was instantly transformed, as the vulgarity and the futility of his life vanished. He was baptized shortly thereafter in the River Ouse, and united with the Baptist church in Bedford, which was pastored by Reverend John Gifford. Shortly after this, in 1655, he entered into the ministry of the Gospel.

It was not long before Bunyan's willingness and drive to preach the Gospel everywhere got him into trouble. By 1660, Anglican royalists had stepped up their attacks on non-conformist preachers (Baptists, Congregationalists, and Puritans in general). It became illegal to preach in non-sanctioned places. So, on November 12, 1660, John Bunyan was arrested for preaching in a field near a farmhouse. Upon his arrest, Bunyan was informed that if he would apologize to the magistrates and refrain from preaching, he would be released. Bunyan replied that such a promise was not possible and thus began a 12-year imprisonment.

These were years of utmost pain and agony for Bunyan. He writes:

> I found myself a man encompassed with infirmities: the parting with my wife and poor children hath often been to me in this place as the pulling of the flesh from my bones...I should have often brought to mind the many hardships, miseries, and wants that my poor family was likely to meet with, should I be taken from them, especially my poor blind child...the thoughts of the hardships my poor blind one might undergo would break my heart to pieces...But yet, recalling myself, thought I, I must venture yon all with God, though it goeth to the quick to leave you.[4]

He did not complain, nor was he idle. He had four occupations. First, he made laces so that his family might have money to live on. Second, he studied the Word of God. He probably memorized most of the Bible by heart during this period. Third, he ministered to the needs of the other prisoners. He spoke with them on a personal basis about their need to trust Christ. In some instances, Bunyan was granted permission to preach to the entire jail. Each opportunity was a gold mine for Bunyan, who

---

4. D.C. Haynes. *The Baptist Denomination.* (New York: Sheldon and Co, 1875) 295.

labored constantly to bring his fellow prisoners to a saving knowledge of Jesus Christ. His fourth occupation was writing books.[5]

During those 12 years of imprisonment, Bunyan wrote *Grace Abounding, Confessions of Faith*, and *A Defense of the Doctrine of Justification by Faith*. Ernest Bacon speculates that it was in the last part of his imprisonment that Bunyan began to formulate his greatest work, *The Pilgrim's Progress*.[6]

Finally, King Charles II released most religious prisoners, including John Bunyan. Bunyan emerged a leader among non-conformists and the pastor of the church at Bedford. He wouldn't have long to spend with his wife and seven children, however. On February 1675, Charles II changed his mind, and Bunyan along with others was arrested again. This time, legally minded friends accomplished the release of Bunyan after a short time. On leaving prison this second time, Bunyan released for publication part one of his monumental The Pilgrims Progress in 1678.

By the time of Bunyan's death in 1688, 11 editions of *The Pilgrim's Progress* had been published with over 100,000 copies in print. He left a legacy of many other great books and poems. None of these, however, are his greatest legacy to us. Bunyan's greatest gift to the Church was his demonstration that the Doctrines of Grace are not static or cold. The Gospel is not predestination—it is Christ! Grace is how God brings us to Christ. Above all, Bunyan loved Christ. He preached Christ and exalted Christ.

"There was first and foremost in John Bunyan a deep personal love for his Savior, the Lord Jesus Christ...Bunyan's books are full of Christ—His welcome, His unshakable truth, His advocacy for sinners....His preaching and writing were Christ-centered, and it was this that carried men's hearts captive to Christ. If our present day preachers and theologians had the same emphasis, a very different spirit would prevail in both the Church and the State."[7]

---

5. *Fighters*, 128-129.
6. Ernest W. Bacon. *John Bunyan: Pilgrim and Dreamer*. (Baker Book House: Grand Rapids, MI, 1983) 118.
7. *John Bunyan: Pilgrim and Dreamer*, 178.

His last days were his best, for he was greatly loved by his people. Even until the end, he was trying to minister to others. Upon hearing of a dispute between a father and son, he rode many miles to intercede. On his way home, he was caught in a terrible storm. By the time he reached his destination, he had caught a tragic fever. Rather than rest, however, he decided to get up and preach the next day; he also finished writing a book, and delivered it to the publishers. A few days later, on August 31, 1688, John Bunyan went home to be with the Lord he had so faithfully served.

The life of John Bunyan is an inspiration to all Christians. He was a mighty preacher, filled with the Holy Spirit. He was a kindly man, always desiring to serve the needs of others. Ultimately, he was a spiritual man. He read his Bible constantly because of his great hunger and desire for a deep knowledge of the mind of God. And this spiritual nature gave him the courage to take a separated stand and not bow the flag of the Gospel to the will of the king. He suffered much, but it was indeed worth it all. He was willing to give all for others.

Truly, John Bunyan had a broken and contrite heart. It was this heart that empowered him to write *The Acceptable Sacrifice*. This persuasive and powerful book was the best ever written by Bunyan and considered by him to be the culmination of his life's work and spiritual understanding.

The **GodChasers.network**, the ministry of Tommy and Jeannie Tenney, is pleased to bring you resources like *The Acceptable Sacrifice* by John Bunyan. This book has been an inspiration to Tommy and countless other GodChasers. If you enjoyed it, you might also enjoy receiving the GodChasers.network monthly newsletter. It's absolutely free! To sign up, just visit our website, write, or call us at:

The GodChasers.network

http://www.GodChasers.net
GodChaser@GodChasers.net

PO Box 3355
Pineville, Louisiana 71361
USA

Voice: (318) 44CHASE (318.442.4273)
Fax: 318.442.6884
Orders: 888.433.3355

We regret that we are only able to send regular postal mailings to US residents at this time. If you live outside of the US, just add your postal address to our mailing list (using the above contact information)—you will automatically begin to receive our mailings as soon as they are available in your area. No matter where you live, you can receive our updates via email! Just provide your email address when you contact us.

1 JB

Duncan Campbell was another historical GodChaser. Known for his instrumental role in the Hebrides Revival, the passion of his message lives on through these audio tapes.

Revival in the Scottish Hebrides
(Three-tape audio series $20)
by Duncan Campbell

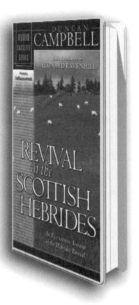

Tape 1 & 2 — Account of the Hebrides Revival: Duncan Campbell describes the power of this awakening as it touched every part of the island. As you listen to his story you will cry out for God to repeat it in our day.

Tape 3 — Ascending the Hill of the Lord: As Moses ascended the hill of the Lord, he lifted the rod of the Lord and assured Israel a great victory. Duncan Campbell, with compelling illustrations from his own ministry, challenges the Church to ascend to the heights of Heaven to bring down a heavenly revival.

Fire on the Altar
(Three-tape audio series $20)
by Duncan Campbell

Tape 1 — Fire of God: As a modern-day Elijah, Duncan Campbell announces that the repair of the broken altar and the cry of the prophetic heart will bring the fire of God into the midst of His people.

Tape 2 — Walking with God: Dr. Campbell leads us to the path where we can take up our walk with God. To reach that place we must learn how to keep in step with the Spirit of the Lord.

Tape 3 — Is the Lord Still Among Us?: Dr. Campbell declares with great confidence that the presence of the Lord will destroy the practices of the devil. When the Lord is among us, demons will flee for fear and men will follow in faith.

2 JB

BOOKS BY *Tommy Tenney*

The Daily Chase: - *$19 (casebound)*
In Hot Pursuit of His Presence

Tommy Tenney has touched the heart of a generation who crave an encounter with their Lord. The passion of his heart, captured in his writings, has ignited a flame of godly pursuit across this world.

The Daily Chase offers you the best of those writings in bite-sized, daily devotional form. Each day there awaits a fresh encounter with the One you long for. Don't hold anything back!

Secret Sources of Power - *$13*

If you are dissatisfied with your life and long for the power of God to work in you, then now is the time to take the keys found in this book and open the door to *Secret Sources of Power.*

God's Favorite House - *$13*

God is looking for a people just like you. He would hush all of Heaven's hosts to listen to your voice raised in heartfelt love songs to Him. This book will show you how to build a house of worship within, fulfilling your heart's desire and His!

The God Chasers - *$12*

What is a God chaser? A person whose hunger exceeds his reach...a person who passion for God's presence presses him to chase the impossible in hopes that the uncatchable migh catch him. Add your name to the list. Come join the ranks of the God chasers.

3 JB

More Fuel
For The Chase!

Holy Hunger - *(Worship CD $15, Cassette $10)*

Jeannie Tenney's much anticipated, long awaited worship album! Recorded live in Australia, this recording includes songs like "Oh Happy Day" and "I'm Hungry For You."

Pursuing His Presence - *(Three-tape audio series $20)*
Tape 1 — Transporting The Glory: There comes a time when God wants us to grow up to another level of maturity. For us, that means walking by the Spirit rather than according to the flesh.
Tape 2 — Turning On The Light Of The Glory: Tommy walks us through the process of unleashing what the body of Christ has always dreamed of: getting to the Glory!

Tape 3 — Building A Mercy Seat: In worship, we create an appropriate environment in which the presence of God can dwell. The focus of the church needs to be reshifted from simply dusting the furniture to building the mercy seat.

Fanning the Flames - *(Three-tape audio series $20)*
Tape 1 — The Application of the Blood and the Ark of the Covenant: Most of the churches in America today dwell in an outer-court experience. Jesus made atonement with His own blood, once for all, and the veil in the temple was rent from top to bottom. Now we have access—come on in!

Tape 2 — A Tale of Two Cities—Nazareth & Nineveh: What city is more likely to experience revival: Nazareth or Nineveh? You might be surprised....
Tape 3 — The "I" Factor: Examine the difference between *ikabod* and *kabod* ("glory"). The arm of flesh cannot achieve what needs to be done. God doesn't need us; we need Him!

From The Anointing To The Glory - *(VHS Video $15)*

Recorded at the Brownsville Revival (Brownsville Assembly of God). The anointing empowers flesh, but the glory disables flesh.

4 JB

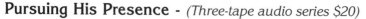